# THE ILLUSTRATED ENCYCLOPEDIA OF
# EXTRAORDINARY AUTOMOBILES

# THE ILLUSTRATED ENCYCLOPEDIA OF
# EXTRAORDINARY AUTOMOBILES

Giles Chapman

# DK

LONDON, NEW YORK, MELBOURNE,
MUNICH, and DELHI

**Managing Editor** Debra Wolter
**Managing Art Editor** Karen Self

**Production Editor** Kavita Varma
**Production Controller** Linda Dare

**Publisher** Jonathan Metcalf
**Art Director** Bryn Walls
**Associate Publisher** Liz Wheeler

Produced for Dorling Kindersley by
**Tall Tree Ltd**

**Editors** Katie Dicker and Jon Richards
**Designer** Ben Ruocco

**US Editor** Chuck Wills

First American Edition, 2009

Published in the United States by
DK Publishing
35 Hudson Street
New York, New York 10014

09 10 11 12 10 9 8 7 6 5 4 3 2

TD347 — May 2009

A CIP catalog record for this book
is available from the Library of Congress

ISBN 978-0-7566-4980-7

DK books are available at special discounts when purchased in bulk for sales
promotions, premiums, fund-raising, or educational use. For details, contact: DK
Publishing Special Markets, 375 Hudson Street, New York, New York 10014 or
SpecialSales@dk.com.

Color reproduction by Colourscan in Singapore

Printed and bound in China by
Hung Hing Offset Printing Company Ltd.

Discover more at
**www.dk.com**

# CONTENTS

## CHAPTER THREE: 1950–1959

# The Jet-Propelled, Chrome-Plated Era 120

## CHAPTER FOUR: 1960–1969

# A Decade Without Limits 202

## CHAPTER FIVE: 1970–1979
## Fuel Crisis and Moon Landings 260

## CHAPTER SIX: 1980 ONWARD
## Driving in a Faster, Cleaner World 302

# 1

## 1885–1929
# THE BIRTH OF INTERNAL COMBUSTION

With a pop and a splutter, the concept of personal transport with its own mobile power source suddenly came to life at the end of the 19th century. German pioneers worked out ways to create "light locomotives"—a leap of imagination that mixed the mobility of the bicycle with miniature versions of the stationary engines then revolutionizing manufacturing industries.

Within 20 years, the "automobile" industry itself was already thriving as, one by one, the design and reliability problems were systematically addressed.

Entrepreneurs could sniff riches and, by 1910, cars were already evolving away from being rich men's playthings into consumer products that were competing for public favor.

With a standardized format of front engine, rear-drive, and a choice of bodywork, the automobile started to radically alter the landscape. The road network, refueling infrastructure, and the very design of our homes evolved to accommodate this brilliant new way to get ourselves where we wanted to be whenever we wanted to go there.

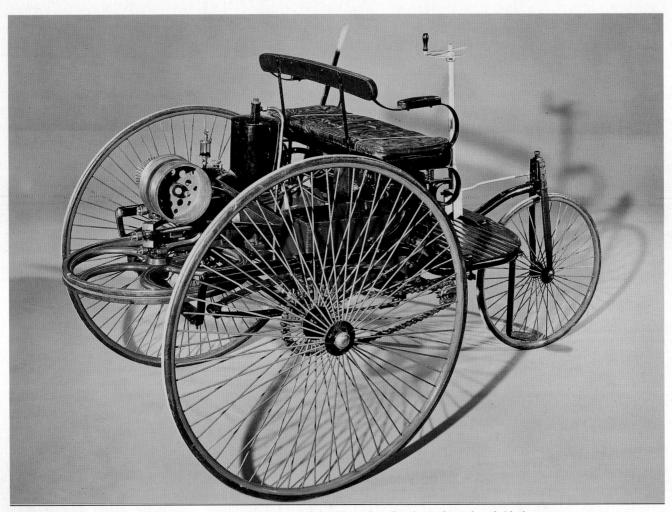

Benz's tricycle, a highly promising technology demonstrator, proved that internal combustion and travel made ideal partners.

# BENZ MOTORWAGEN

Although many automotive pioneers helped to shape the modern car, only Karl Benz actually "invented" it. His "Motorwagen" was made official in 1886, after his patents were registered. However, his spindly three-wheeler, with its single-cylinder, four-stroke internal gas combustion engine, spluttered into life on the roads of Mannheim, Germany, the previous year.

By a stroke of coincidence, Canstatt engineer Gottlieb Daimler had also designed a "high-speed" internal combustion powerplant in 1885. His motor ran on gas, but he chose to install it in a primitive motorcycle for demonstrations.

Many years later, in 1926, the Daimler and Benz companies merged to form Mercedes-Benz. Yet there is no record of Karl Benz and Gottlieb Daimler ever having met (the latter died in 1900). Furthermore, their approaches to self-propelled vehicles were contrasting. Apart from the different fuels used initially, Benz was not, at first, as progressive as his rival whose hot-tube ignition system better suited a mobile engine with its own portable supply of spirits. Daimler's first car-like prototype of 1886 also provided the additional wheel that most car drivers quickly came to expect.

On the other hand, Benz put an improved version of his tiller-steered tricycle on sale in 1888 (no regular production Daimler was on sale until 1892). Moreover, by 1893, his newly-designed Benz Velo became the world's first production car. A transportation revolution was beginning.

## SPECIFICATION

**YEAR REVEALED**  1885

**PLACE OF ORIGIN**
Mannheim, Germany

**HISTORICAL STATUS**
prototype—the first "car"

**ENGINE**  single-cylinder, 58ci (954cc)

**MAXIMUM POWER**  0.9bhp

**LAYOUT**  rear-mounted engine driving the rear wheels

**BODYWORK**  none

**TOP SPEED**  10mph (16kph)

**NUMBER BUILT**  one

*"In those days when our little boat of life threatened to capsize, only one person stood steadfastly by me, my wife. She bravely set new sails of hope."*

KARL BENZ, WRITING IN HIS AUTOBIOGRAPHY

Benz's 1886 patent for a "vehicle with gasoline-engine propulsion."

# LANCHESTER

The first-ever, all-British gasoline car took to the road in Birmingham in December 1895, when Frederick Lanchester fired up his prototype and eased it forward those first, historic feet.

Fred had designed the whole thing from scratch, including the centrally located single-cylinder engine. It had a three-speed gearbox, and was steered by an upright tiller. Its cantilever spring suspension and torsionally stiff chassis gave—for the times—an astounding ride. It could also do 15mph (24kph)—highly illegal at a time when cars were governed at 4mph (6kph) with an escort.

What it couldn't do was get up hills very well. Driver and passenger were both obliged to get out and help it up all but the gentlest slopes. That didn't deter the young British maverick, however. Two years later, a new, more powerful and superbly balanced 214ci (3,500cc) twin-cylinder engine was installed. The car could now reach 18mph (29kph).

In 1899, the Lanchester Engine Company was formed with plans to make a production car. This was easily feasible because the scrupulous Lanchester had created interchangeable components between each of his prototypes.

## SPECIFICATION

**YEAR REVEALED** 1895

**PLACE OF ORIGIN** Birmingham, UK

**HISTORICAL STATUS** prototype

**ENGINE** single-cylinder, 80ci (1,306cc)

**MAXIMUM POWER** 5bhp

**LAYOUT** mid-mounted engine driving the rear wheels

**BODYWORK** six-seater open tourer

**TOP SPEED** 15mph (24kph)

**NUMBER BUILT** one

*"He was a perfectionist, but he was unconventional and obstinate in his approach. He didn't suffer fools gladly and lesser people found it hard to catch up with him."*

CHRIS CLARK, LANCHESTER HISTORIAN, SPEAKING ABOUT FREDERICK LANCHESTER

This Lanchester, Britain's first-ever car, was amazingly sophisticated for the time, but steep hills were still a struggle.

Along with his friend Jim Bishop, Henry Ford burned the midnight oil to build this, his first car, which managed without any brakes at all.

# FORD "QUADRICYCLE"

The neighbors might not have realized it, but there was something of a "Eureka!" moment at 58 Bagley Avenue, Detroit in the early hours of June 4, 1896. At about 4am, Henry Ford's first car clattered into life and set off on its maiden journey along the city's dark and deserted streets. He was led by his friend Jim Bishop, riding a bicycle.

The tiny four-wheeled, single-seater contraption—the "Quadricycle"—was the result of considerable effort for Ford, then chief engineer of the Edison Illuminating Company. He built his first engine in 1893, and had spent every spare hour building a car for it ever since.

In contrast to other early car-making attempts, Ford's vehicle was extremely light. Only the engine, wheels, axles, and steering rod were metal—the rest of the structure was wooden—keeping weight down to just 500lb (227kg). The chain-driven transmission was a first. There were two speeds available, giving maximums of 10 or 20mph (16 or 32kph), selected by twin drive belts that could be engaged by a floor-mounted clutch. There was no reverse gear, however, and no brakes at all.

The very first "Ford" car had proved that the new technology could be made on a scale many times smaller than the other key self-propelled vehicles of the day—railroad locomotives. But it was only the beginning for Henry Ford, who immediately set about refining the Quadricycle, substituting many of its wooden parts with sturdier metal components.

> ## SPECIFICATION
>
> **YEAR REVEALED** 1896
>
> **PLACE OF ORIGIN** Detroit, Michigan
>
> **HISTORICAL STATUS** prototype
>
> **ENGINE** flat two-cylinder, 59ci (970cc)
>
> **MAXIMUM POWER** 10bhp
>
> **LAYOUT** mid-mounted engine driving the rear wheels
>
> **BODYWORK** none
>
> **TOP SPEED** 20mph (32kph)
>
> **NUMBER BUILT** one

*"I cannot say that it was hard work. No work with interest is ever hard."*

HENRY FORD

Ford's flat-twin engine drove the rear wheels via a chain.

The irascible, bearded Jenatzy on board his rocket-like record car, a shining early example of an advanced electric car.

# JENATZY "LA JAMAIS CONTENTE"

You can probably blame the French count Gaston de Chasseloup-Laubat for our global obsession with covering ground as quickly as possible. In 1898, he drove his rickety Jeantaud electric car on a stretch of road near Paris, and was thrilled when timekeepers confirmed that he had reached a speed of 39.24mph (63.15kph).

As no one had been officially timed driving an automobile at quite such a gallop, he established the first "world land speed record." Records of course, are there to be broken, and throughout 1899, the count saw fierce rivalry from Camille Jenatzy.

The engineer son of a Belgian fabric manufacturer, Jenatzy had experience in making electric taxicabs. However, for his record car, which he christened "La Jamais Contente" (The Never Satisfied), he commissioned a special cigar-shaped body from the Rothschild coachwork company.

The body was made of aluminum to cut swiftly through the airflow, and the car rode on Michelin pneumatic tires. The power came from two 25kw electric motors, whose 200-volt output gave the equivalent of about 68bhp.

The land speed record was traded between the two adventurers. Finally, Jenatzy (nicknamed the Red Devil because of the color of his beard) defeated his rival for good. La Jamais Contente established a record of 65.79mph (105.88kph) on May 1, 1899, at Acheres, Yvelines, just outside Paris. This record remained until 1902, when it was swiped by a steam-powered Serpollet car.

## SPECIFICATION

**YEAR REVEALED**  1899

**PLACE OF ORIGIN**  Paris, France

**HISTORICAL STATUS**  speed record car

**ENGINE**  two 25kw electric motors

**MAXIMUM POWER**  68bhp equivalent

**LAYOUT**  front-mounted engines driving the rear wheels

**BODYWORK**  single-seater "torpedo"

**TOP SPEED**  65mph (105kph)

**NUMBER BUILT**  one

*"As an illustration of his irascible temperament, it is related that during one race he jumped from his car and struck an inoffensive onlooker whose demeanor displeased him."*

NEW YORK TIMES, 1913, REPORTING JENATZY'S DEATH IN A HUNTING ACCIDENT

With its wheelhub-mounted electric motors, the Lohner-Porsche offered four-wheel drive, and the first gas-electric hybrid drive system.

# LOHNER-PORSCHE

The Porsche name first hit the headlines in 1900, when a groundbreaking new vehicle was unveiled at the World Exhibition in Paris. The 24-year-old Austrian-born engineer Ferdinand Porsche was already showing his brilliance, in this case with electric power.

At the time, electric cars were just as popular as gas-fueled vehicles. The Lohner coachbuilding company of Vienna, a business favored by local nobility, decided to get involved. It had already built a handful of electric machines when Porsche joined the company and persuaded them to make his "Radnabenmotor."

The vehicle did away with any kind of complicated transmission and bulky driveshaft by turning an electric motor into a wheel hub itself. With two of these at the front, the upright Lohner was a nimble front-wheel drive car.

Porsche then created the Lohner Mixte—without doubt the world's first hybrid car. The Mixte added a small gas engine, connected directly to an 80-volt dynamo. This acted as an onboard generator; as it moved along, it produced electricity to power the wheel-mounted motors.

However, in Porsche's ultimate version of the car, a quartet of these electric wheel units gave a very early form of four-wheel drive. Any shortcomings that the car's transmission might have had were probably not obvious on the poor road surfaces. As a surefooted device for negotiating mountain roads, it was little short of sensational.

## SPECIFICATION

**YEAR REVEALED** 1899

**PLACE OF ORIGIN** Vienna, Austria

**HISTORICAL STATUS**
production car

**ENGINE** electric motors and also
gas-electric hybrid

**MAXIMUM POWER** unknown

**LAYOUT** wheel-mounted electric
motors driving the front wheels;
rear-mounted engine powering electric
motors in all wheels

**BODYWORK** two- or four-seater
open tourer

**TOP SPEED** unknown

**NUMBER BUILT** unknown

*"He [Ferdinand Porsche] is very young but is a man with a big career before him. You will hear from him again."* JACOB LOHNER

Lohner-Porsche badge

The fascinating array of vehicles at a
motor and bicycle exhibition, held at
London's Olympia Exhibition Hall just
after the turn of the 20th century. You
can see the huge variety of forms that
early motorized-transport could take,
with drivers and passengers seated in a
bewildering number of configurations,
most of which took scant regard for safety.

# OLDSMOBILE "CURVED DASH"

Two important things held back car sales in their earliest days. One, obviously, was price: these new toys were prohibitively expensive for most. The other was mistrust—people often felt happier traveling by horse, and many were only just getting to grips with the idea of the bicycle.

The Olds Motor Works of Detroit, Michigan, however, sought to tackle both these issues. Founded by Ransom E. Olds, the company came up with a small car in 1901 for just $650—still expensive, but within many people's grasp. Lights, mudguards, and a hood were fitted at extra cost. They called it the Oldsmobile.

Such an attractive price was possible because of Olds' novel adoption of a mass-production system. Making the car from standardized parts in an efficient factory layout meant costs could be lowered dramatically.

A key spur to the Oldsmobile's popularity was its resemblance to a two-seater horse-drawn buggy. Its characteristic curved-dash panel at the front provided its nickname. The rear-mounted, water-cooled, single-cylinder engine was gravity-fed from a brass carburetor, and there was a semi-automatic, two-speed-and-reverse transmission. Steering was by simple tiller, and two huge springs provided the suspension.

The Oldsmobile was the first car to gain the true affection of the American public. It rapidly gained an excellent reputation for reliability, and was widely exported, even as far as Moscow in Russia.

## SPECIFICATION

**YEAR REVEALED** 1901

**PLACE OF ORIGIN** Lansing, Michigan

**HISTORICAL STATUS** production car

**ENGINE** single-cylinder, 96ci (1,565cc)

**MAXIMUM POWER** 7bhp

**LAYOUT** rear-mounted engine driving the rear wheels

**BODYWORK** two-seater open buggy

**TOP SPEED** 19mph (31kph)

**NUMBER BUILT** approximately 19,000

*"To the church we'll swiftly steal, Then our wedding bells will peal. You can go as far as you like with me, In my Merry Oldsmobile."*

VINCENT P. BRYAN'S LYRIC FROM *IN MY MERRY OLDSMOBILE*, A POPULAR SONG IN 1905

An affordable price and mechanical simplicity endeared the Oldsmobile to America; you can see the "curved dash" that gave the car its nickname.

# STANLEY STEAMER

A steam-powered car seems anachronistic today, but when identical twins F. E. and F. O. Stanley began making them in 1897, it was the most proven motive technology around.

Early Stanley cars featured a tubular chassis frame with a light, wooden buggy body. The vertical boiler, under the double seat, at first featured copper fire tubes, with a vapourizing gasoline burner underneath. Drive went from the engine crankshaft to a rear-mounted differential, by chain.

The design was a success and soon the company was bought by a business consortium for $250,000. But the new owners lacked the Stanleys' touch, and the brothers bought their old factory back in 1901 for just $20,000.

They immediately put an improved model, the definitive Stanley Steamer, into production. It featured a new, horizontally mounted engine, geared direct to the back axle. And the boiler was later shifted to the front.

The Steamer's finest hour came in 1906, when Fred Marriott drove a special one across Daytona Beach, Florida, at 127.659mph (205.447kph)—still the longest-standing unbroken record for steam-powered cars, over a century

## SPECIFICATION

**YEAR REVEALED** 1901

**PLACE OF ORIGIN** Newton, Massachusetts

**HISTORICAL STATUS** production car

**ENGINE** twin-cylinder, 89ci (1,460cc)

**MAXIMUM POWER** 4.5bhp

**LAYOUT** mid/front-mounted engine driving the rear wheels

**BODYWORK** 2+2 open "runabout" tourer

**TOP SPEED** 35mph (56kph)

**NUMBER BUILT** 1,500 (up to 1904)

*"On a cold day, there are huge clouds of steam behind me, which people often confuse with smoke and then swear at me."*    JEY LENO, STANLEY STEAMER OWNER

Steam was a viable source of power in motoring's early times, and the Stanley brothers' cars were among the most popular.

# MERCEDES 60HP

Before the new generation of Mercedes was unveiled in 1901, cars had come in a bewildering plethora of configurations—many of them related to the horse-drawn coach. In 1886, Gottlieb Daimler built the world's first four-wheeled car by adapting such an item.

In 1898–99, Daimler and his colleague Wilhelm Maybach, also built a racing machine—the 28hp Canstatt-Daimler—that was typically short and top-heavy.

One was bought by Emile Jellinek, an Austro-Hungarian diplomat and entrepreneur. Although he found its dynamics decidedly wanting, he told the Daimler partners if they came up with a design for both racing and touring, he'd buy three dozen. In exchange for exclusive rights, he'd also sell more under his Mercedes brand (after Mercedes Jellinek, his 11-year-old daughter.)

Gottlieb Daimler died in 1900, but Maybach suggested a car already envisaged with Paul Daimler, Gottlieb's eldest son. The Mercedes 35hp was truly revolutionary in its packaging. Cradled by a pressed-steel chassis frame, occupants sat behind a four-cylinder engine. Its lowered center of gravity vastly improved driveability and roadholding, and in 1903, two years after the first model had been shown, the closely related Mercedes 60hp sat at the top of the range. No matter what form of magnificent coachwork it carried, the car was by some measure the most advanced vehicle on the market, and immediately inspired imitators.

## SPECIFICATION

**YEAR REVEALED** 1903

**PLACE OF ORIGIN** Bad Canstatt, Germany

**HISTORICAL STATUS** production car

**ENGINE** four-cylinder, 564ci (9,235cc)

**MAXIMUM POWER** 60bhp

**LAYOUT** front-mounted engine driving the rear wheels

**BODYWORK** various custom-made tourers and saloons

**TOP SPEED** 56mph (90kph)

**NUMBER BUILT** Unknown

*"The name of my daughter has certain publicity characteristics that would be lost by using some other name. The name is both exotic and attractive."*

EMILE JELLINEK, 1900, ON HIS CHOICE OF THE MERCEDES BRAND

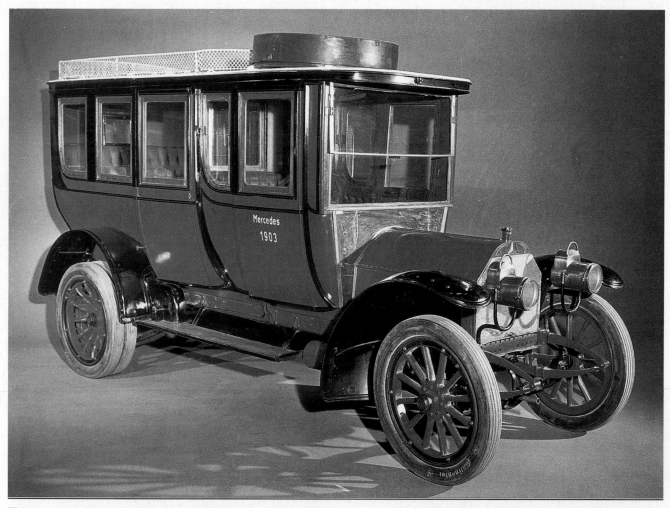

This imposing and commodious body on a Mercedes 60hp chassis might have been used by a large, wealthy family, or as a hotel limousine.

The Rolls-Royce 40/50hp Silver Ghost was certainly one of the world's finest contemporary cars, beloved of landed gentry and sporting gentlemen.

# ROLLS-ROYCE "SILVER GHOST"

The new Rolls-Royce 40/50hp chassis was launched at London's Olympia Motor Show in 1906. It was designed by Henry Royce to meet the demand from Edwardian motorists for a car to carry the epitome of luxurious coachwork.

Thought to be the 12th built, the very chassis on display was fitted with elegant silver-painted "Roi-des-Belges" touring coachwork and silver-plated brightwork by coachbuilder Barker & Co. It was to be used as a "trials car" by the company's managing director Claude Johnson. Johnson called his new Rolls-Royce "The Silver Ghost."

It had a six-cylinder engine and an overdrive fourth speed (the "sprinting gear"). This was adventurous when most motorists were still reluctant to change gear.

In May 1907, the Silver Ghost began a series of public tests, culminating in an observed 15,000-mile (24,000-km) run. Over six weeks, Johnson and a team of three drivers, including the Hon Charles Rolls, covered nearly 2,500 miles (4,023 kilometers) a week, running around the clock, and only halting to change tires.

At the end of the test, the RAC stripped the car to measure wear: the cost of replacement parts amounted to just £2 2s 7d, although tire costs totaled £187 12s 6d.

The trial made such an impression on the motoring public that the name "Silver Ghost" became indiscriminately used for all Rolls-Royce 40/50s. The company proudly adopted the slogan, first used in *The Times* newspaper: "The Best Car in the World."

## SPECIFICATION

**YEAR REVEALED** 1906

**PLACE OF ORIGIN** Manchester, UK

**HISTORICAL STATUS**
production car

**ENGINE** six-cylinder, 429ci (7,036cc)

**MAXIMUM POWER** 48bhp

**LAYOUT** front-mounted engine
driving the rear wheels

**BODYWORK** various custom-made
tourers and limousines

**TOP SPEED** 55mph (89kph)

**NUMBER BUILT** 6,173

*"At whatever speed this car is being driven... there is no engine so far as sensation goes, nor are one's auditory nerves troubled, driving or standing, by a fuller sound than emanates from an eight-day clock."*

THE AUTOCAR MAGAZINE, 1907

Rolls-Royce quality was already legion, and the guarantee backed that up.

# FORD MODEL T

Henry Ford had one ultimate aim for his Ford Motor Company: he wanted to make a rugged car of a standard design that could be built in high numbers at low prices. Out of this policy came the Model T, and a revolution in 20th-century manufacturing.

Extensive use of vanadium and heat-treated steel made the car light but sturdy (hence its nickname "Tin Lizzie"), with 10.5in (27cm) of road clearance, and hefty suspension to cope with rough roads. The drivetrain was enclosed to keep out dust, and the Model T was 6.9ft (2.1m) tall. Ford and his colleagues created a manufacturing colossus that began feeding a production line in Detroit.

Employees added parts to Model Ts as they slowly rolled past them. A year later, Fords accounted for half of all American cars built.

"Any color," Henry Ford is often quoted as saying, "as long as it's black." In truth, the Model T did originally come in other colors until the introduction of moving-line mass-production. After that, "Japan black" was standardized because it was cheap and durable. In 1926, a choice of colors returned to the Model T for its final two years after the introduction of quick-drying cellulose lacquer paint.

Indeed, assembly took place all around the world, and by the time the Model T ended its incredible 19-year life in 1927, 15,007,033 models had been made.

## SPECIFICATION

**YEAR REVEALED** 1908

**PLACE OF ORIGIN** Detroit, US

**HISTORICAL STATUS**
production car

**ENGINE** four-cylinder, 177ci (2,896cc)

**MAXIMUM POWER** 20bhp

**LAYOUT** front-mounted engine driving the rear wheels

**BODYWORK** two-seater runabout or coupé, four-seater tourer, seven-seater landaulette/saloon

**TOP SPEED** 40mph (64kph)

**NUMBER BUILT** 15,007,033

*"It is without doubt the greatest creation in automobiles ever placed before a people."*

A FORD DEALER, COMMENTING ON THE MODEL T

This copy of Ford's house magazine reinforces the universal nature of the Model T.

The Model T always boasted a high-ground clearance among its sturdy attributes, making it well-suited to the state of roads in 1920s America.

Vauxhall paid great attention to detail for its **KN**, but only got it past **100mph** (161kph) by draining it of all but essential oil, to save weight.

# VAUXHALL KN

Before World War II, Vauxhall, still very much with us today as General Motors' British subsidiary, was as eager as any maker of sports cars to prove its products on the racetrack. At the newly opened Brooklands circuit in Surrey, the company wanted to show that a relatively "ordinary" car could reach the magic figure of 161kph (100mph).

The company's tiny Experimental Shop team transformed the 20hp A-type, a typical medium-sized car of the day, into a speed machine. They came up with the KN, designed to cheat the wind with its tube body and disc wheels. A radiator mounted sideways-on was kept cool via plentiful louvers in the hood, although the hot air that blew back into the cockpit was no fun for the driver. Tests were promising and, after much modification, the Vauxhall team turned up at Brooklands in October 1910 for their assault on "the ton" (100mph). Vauxhall works manager AJ Hancock was at the wheel. The best they could manage was 99.5mph (160kph) until it was suggested that draining the gearbox and rear axle of all but a splash of oil, would reduce weight. The happy result was an official 1-kilometer (0.62-mile) speed of 100.08mph (161.06kph).

As a niche manufacturer, Vauxhall was making around 200 cars a year at the time, and the KN paved the way for the launch of its Prince Henry and 30/98 sports cars in subsequent years. However, after General Motors took over in 1925, the era of handmade thoroughbreds and sporting success soon gave way to mass-production.

## SPECIFICATION

**YEAR REVEALED** 1909

**PLACE OF ORIGIN** Luton, Bedfordshire, UK

**HISTORICAL STATUS** speed record car

**ENGINE** four-cylinder, 186ci (3,053cc)

**MAXIMUM POWER** 20bhp

**LAYOUT** front-mounted engine driving the rear wheels

**BODYWORK** single-seater racer

**TOP SPEED** 100mph (161kph)

**NUMBER BUILT** one

*"Like cayenne pepper, it was hot stuff."*

RUDOLF SELZ, VAUXHALL DIRECTOR AND RACING DRIVER ON THE KN

# FIAT S76 300HP

The quest for ultimate speed has led to some bizarre-looking machines—none more so than Fiat's elephantine S76. Built in 1911, it tried to wrest the land speed record away from Germany's "Blitzen Benz."

The Italian engineers reckoned there could be no substitute for engine capacity, as demonstrated by the Benz's 1,281ci (21,000cc). They came up with a monumental overhead-valve engine of 1,730ci (28,353cc)that produced its 300bhp at 1,800rpm, yet still employed just four cylinders. The engine was so tall the driver had to almost peer around the edge of the hood, but to aid aerodynamics, it was extremely narrow.

The S76 was dispatched to Britain's Brooklands circuit where it was put through its paces by intrepid factory driver Pietro Bordino. After a subsequent journey on public roads, it thundered to a best speed of 116mph (187kph) at Saltburn Sands, Middlesborough—setting the record for the fastest flying mile time.

Fiat was satisfied, but Prince Boris Sukhanov, a wealthy Russian, was hooked on the enormous vehicle. He is thought to have acquired one of the two cars made, but too timid to drive it himself, he sponsored a record run with French driver Arthur Duray at Ostend, Belgium. It was said to have reached 137mph (220kph), but suspect timing equipment and bad weather prevented two runs within an hour—a requirement for a world record qualification. Sukhanov's team spent a further six weeks trying in late 1913 before admitting defeat.

---

## SPECIFICATION

**YEAR REVEALED** 1911

**PLACE OF ORIGIN** Turin, Italy

**HISTORICAL STATUS** speed record car

**ENGINE** four-cylinder, 1,730ci (28,353cc)

**MAXIMUM POWER** 300bhp

**LAYOUT** front-mounted engine driving the rear wheels

**BODYWORK** two-seater racer

**TOP SPEED** 137mph (220kph)

**NUMBER BUILT** two

---

*"These power plants were used in aircraft as well as for automobile racing. They are as beautiful on paper as in reality."*

FROM *FIAT 1899–1989: AN ITALIAN INDUSTRIAL REVOLUTION*, A BOOK TO ACCOMPANY THE EPONYMOUS EXHIBITION AT THE SCIENCE MUSEUM, LONDON, IN 1989

With one of the most enormous conventional car engines of all time, seeing over the towering hood of the Fiat S76 was a challenge to drivers.

This Gyrocar is standing up on two wheels with four people on board, but its huge turning circle was something of a hindrance when parking.

# SCHILOVSKI GYROCAR

Recently described by Stephen Vokins of Britain's National Motor Museum as "a fantastic answer to a question no-one had asked," the Gyrocar was an attempt to marry car and motorcycle. To make up for the balance usually bestowed on a two-wheeler by its rider, the Gyrocar used a huge gyroscope to keep it upright—quite a task for the 2.7-ton five-seater contraption.

It was the brainchild of Russian aristocrat and lawyer Count Peter Schilovski, who contracted Britain's Wolseley Tool & Motor Car Company to build it. Some 10 percent of the engine's output was devoted to powering a dynamo and electric motor. This kept the substantial, 40in- (102cm-) diameter gyroscope spinning at between 2–3,000rpm. An alarm bell rang if rotating speed dropped too low to keep the "car" upright, and tiny support wheels were automatically lowered either side to stop it toppling over.

Despite a vast turning circle, the Gyrocar worked, and could reverse and partly maneuver like any conventional four-wheeler. It caused a sensation when demonstrated to crowds in London's Regent's Park in April 1914.

Improbably, the Count planned to sell his patented Gyrocar technology to the Russian Army, claiming such vehicles could cross rough ground far faster than a four-wheeler, and use less fuel to do so. However, mistakenly thinking the Count had perished in the Russian Revolution (he actually settled in London), Wolseley directors made the bizarre decision to bury the Gyrocar.

## SPECIFICATION

**YEAR REVEALED** 1912

**PLACE OF ORIGIN** Birmingham, UK

**HISTORICAL STATUS** prototype

**ENGINE** four-cylinder, 188ci (3,080cc)

**MAXIMUM POWER** 20bhp

**LAYOUT** front-mounted engine driving the rear wheel

**BODYWORK** five-seater open tourer

**TOP SPEED** unknown

**NUMBER BUILT** one

*"We drove the car backwards and forwards for a distance of about six feet many times. During these tests it was noticeable that one could stand on the side of the car and step into the body without any disturbance of balance."*

FROM A REPORT BY A. W. DRING, WOLSELEY CHIEF EXPERIMENTAL ENGINEER

# ALFA ROMEO 40-60HP AERODINAMICA

The Italian count Mario Ricotti turned out to be quite a visionary. His idea that popular cars of the future would be highly aerodynamic "one box" people carriers was extraordinarily prescient.

When Count Ricotti commissioned this stunning machine from the Italian coachbuilder Carrozzeria Castagna, he was said to be in awe of the fashionable airships of that period.

The teardrop lines of the one-off car are softly profiled, with the wind-cheating front section completely enclosing the engine, and the tail coming to a tapered end of masterful proportion. The bodywork was made from riveted-aluminum paneling,

Alfa Romeo badge

while the elongated windshield section at the front consisted of three separate pieces of curved glass.

The limits of contemporary technology, however, were clearly visible. The substantial side-members and primitive suspension of the 40-60hp are obvious. With the engine and radiator inside the body's contours, the driver had to sit over three feet behind the windshield, with visibility impeded by the side windows.

Ricotti may have been eccentric, but he wasn't stupid. When he grew tired of his new toy, he removed the body and had an open tourer built on the chassis. The body itself survives in Alfa Romeo's Museo Storico.

## SPECIFICATION

**YEAR REVEALED**  1914

**PLACE OF ORIGIN**  Milan, Italy

**HISTORICAL STATUS**  prototype

**ENGINE**  four-cylinder, 371ci (6,082cc)

**MAXIMUM POWER**  70bhp

**LAYOUT**  front-mounted engine driving the rear wheels

**BODYWORK**  single-door, five-seater saloon

**TOP SPEED**  86mph (138kph)

**NUMBER BUILT**  one

*"Seemingly an escapee from a Jules Verne novel, this extraordinary vehicle had a streamlined fuselage like that of an aircraft, pierced with large portholes."*

SERGE BELLU, FRENCH CAR HISTORIAN AND ILLUSTRATOR

The profile of the Castagna-built Aerodinamica body was truly astounding for 1914, although the stout, old-fashioned chassis is clearly visible.

Conceived as a "real car in miniature," the Austin Seven offered four cylinders and four seats; the automotive foundation for BMW.

# AUSTIN SEVEN

Herbert Austin quit Wolseley in 1905 to set up his own company, called Austin, and by the early 1920s it was one of Britain's most important carmakers with 22,000 employees. But it was not all plain sailing.

The company struggled after World War I, as the inevitable financial downturn bit hard, and Austin's stately 20hp models suffered when tax penalties were levied on them in Britain's "Motor Car Act" of 1920. Turnover fell and Austin's company briefly operated under administrators.

Clearly a big idea was needed. Salvation came along when Austin proposed to "motorize the common man" with a very small, economical car. He might have been inspired by the many cheap-to-buy "cyclecars" being offered by enterprising French companies, but this type of flimsy device wasn't quite what he had in mind. Instead, he wanted to make a car in miniature, with none of the compromises of using motorcycle parts. Yet, it would have to sell for about the same as a motorbike-sidecar combination.

Despite scorn from his co-directors, Austin worked with a talented 18-year-old draftsman called Stanley Edge. Together they created what became the Austin Seven. Unveiled in 1922 at £165, the Austin Seven offered four seats, a four-cylinder engine, and four-wheel brakes.

The Seven instantly became the world's leading small car. Rights were sold worldwide and it was brazenly copied in Japan for the first Datsun.

## SPECIFICATION

**YEAR REVEALED** 1922

**PLACE OF ORIGIN** Birmingham, UK

**HISTORICAL STATUS** production car

**ENGINE** four-cylinder, 42ci (696cc)

**MAXIMUM POWER** 10bhp

**LAYOUT** front-mounted engine driving the rear wheels

**BODYWORK** two-door, four-seater tourer

**TOP SPEED** 40mph (64kph)

**NUMBER BUILT** 302,000

*"He [Herbert Austin] was hellishly bad-tempered. I only learned later that he was having quite a battle with his directors to get money allocated for the Seven."*

STANLEY EDGE, AUSTIN SEVEN DESIGNER

# LANCIA LAMBDA

The concept of a new car "bristling" with the latest technology is often bandied about, but few new models carried as much all-round innovation at their debut as Lancia's sporty Lambda. It broke new ground in its engine, its suspension, and its overall construction.

Vincenzo Lancia was inspired by shipbuilding principles for the Lambda concept. From a structural viewpoint, it was the first car to do away with a separate chassis frame altogether. Its rigid monocoque unit was a pressed-steel skeleton forming the chassis, scuttle, lower body, and rear end, while the engine was carried in a cradle of riveted crossmembers and light tubes. Holes were cut in non-load-bearing areas to save weight.

The Lambda's single overhead-camshaft engine was the first to successfully enter mass-production, its aluminum pistons and block being a very bold move for the Italian company. But the independent front suspension was a breakthrough, too.

The combination of excellent rigidity in the body, the carefully weighted front end, and the compactness of the power unit, gave the Lambda new standards of roadholding. It made contemporary alternatives seem positively unwieldy by comparison. Although its integral construction meant buyers had to accept the factory's own style of coachwork, a "bare chassis" version was developed in 1925. A later sedan option was offered in the form of an enormous, detachable hardtop.

## SPECIFICATION

**YEAR REVEALED** 1922

**PLACE OF ORIGIN** Turin, Italy

**HISTORICAL STATUS**
production car

**ENGINE** V4-cylinder, 129ci (2,121cc)

**MAXIMUM POWER** 49bhp

**LAYOUT** front-mounted engine
driving the rear wheels

**BODYWORK** four-door,
five-seater tourer

**TOP SPEED** 70mph (113kph)

**NUMBER BUILT**
approximately 11,200

*"Sgr. Lancia intends to design a car which will carry the mechanical units without using the classical frame; I am filled with enthusiasm."*

BATTISTA FALCHETTO, LANCIA ENGINEER WHO WORKED ON THE LAMBDA

Hollywood actress Greta Garbo and friend take an exhilarating trip in a Lancia Lambda, one of the most advanced cars of the Flapper era.

# HIGHAM-THOMAS "BABS" SPECIAL

John Godfrey Parry-Thomas was an outstanding engineer born in Wrexham, North Wales, in 1885. In 1917, he was appointed chief engineer of Leyland Motors Ltd. He patented electrical transmission systems, the Thomas piston, and designed an advanced luxury car, the Leyland Eight.

When plans to manufacture the Leyland Eight were axed, Thomas decided to set up as an independent. In 1923, he established his own small factory at Brooklands circuit, in Surrey, where he already enjoyed a growing reputation as a racing driver. He also nurtured an ambition to take the land speed record. Thomas's break came when he bought one of of Count Zborowski's unfinished "Chitty-Chitty-Bang-Bang" cars for just £125. Officially, it became the "Higham Special", powered by a stupendous 1,581ci (25,900cc), V12 Liberty aero engine, but it was soon re-christened "Babs."

Thomas made his first assault on the record with Babs in 1925 on Pendine Sands in South Wales. It was not to his satisfaction so the car returned to Brooklands for a new body and reworked engine. In April 1926, again at Pendine, Thomas pushed it to 169.30mph (272.46kph) and then, the very next day, to 171.02mph (275.23kph).

Malcolm Campbell broke the record the following February. A month later, suffering from flu, Thomas unofficially bettered 180mph (290kph) at Pendine when one of the drivechains snapped. Babs crashed and caught fire, but Thomas was already dead—fatally wounded by the flailing chain.

## SPECIFICATION

**YEAR REVEALED** 1923–25

**PLACE OF ORIGIN** Higham, Kent, and Byfleet, Surrey, UK

**HISTORICAL STATUS** speed record car

**ENGINE** V12-cylinder, 1,581ci (25,900cc)

**MAXIMUM POWER** 450bhp

**LAYOUT** front-mounted engine driving the rear wheels

**BODYWORK** single-seater racer

**TOP SPEED** 180mph (290kph)

**NUMBER BUILT** one

*"Sick Man Whom Doctor Warned of Risk. Defied After Effects of Influenza to Win Back Lost Laurels with Favourite Babs Car."*

*DAILY MIRROR (UK)* HEADLINES ON MARCH 27, 1927

"Babs" was, briefly, the fastest car on earth. The car lay buried in the sands at Pendine until it was dug up in 1969 and restored.

Mechanics inspect the Bluebird's engine prior to the world record attempt with Campbell (in plus-fours) keeping a watchful eye.

# SUNBEAM 350HP "BLUEBIRD"

The battle for the world land speed record entered an extraordinary phase in 1922 when aircraft engines became the favored method to push the boundaries of speed.

The 1,118ci (18,322cc), V12 Sunbeam Manitou engine saw active service in only one airplane before being used in powerboats. In 1920, however, an engine was installed in a Sunbeam chassis, to produce a car with record-breaking capabilities.

Redesigned to produce 350hp—50 more than in aircraft form—the engine was given shaft-drive to the rear wheels—much safer than the dangerous chains that could sometimes break and injure the driver.

In 1922, Kenelm Lee Guinness made land speed history at Brooklands when he drove the Sunbeam to a record-breaking 133.75mph (215.25kph). Next it was the turn of dedicated speed freak Malcolm Campbell, who touched 138mph (222kph) at Saltburn, North Yorkshire, although a faulty stopwatch prevented him from becoming the fastest driver on earth. However, Campbell was smitten with the car and persuaded Sunbeam to sell it to him. He painted it blue and named it "Bluebird."

Campbell eventually took the land speed record after the car had received crucial aerodynamic modifications: in September 1924, at Pendine Sands in South Wales, he achieved the official time of 146.16mph (235.22kph). Later, Campbell would use the Sunbeam to become the first man to drive at a speed of more than 150mph (240kph).

## SPECIFICATION

**YEAR REVEALED** 1924

**PLACE OF ORIGIN** Wolverhampton, UK

**HISTORICAL STATUS** speed record car

**ENGINE** V12-cylinder, 1,118ci (18,322cc)

**MAXIMUM POWER** 350bhp

**LAYOUT** front-mounted engine driving the rear wheels

**BODYWORK** single-seater racer

**TOP SPEED** 152mph (245kph)

**NUMBER BUILT** one

*"Happiness is by the side of each and every one of us, always within reach, yet if pursued to catch and possess is beyond our grasp."*

SIR MALCOLM CAMPBELL

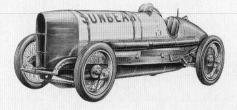

The Monotrace was nominally a two-wheeler "car," although it had drop-down stabilizer wheels for stationary moments.

# MONOTRACE

A two-wheeled car was what the Monotrace purported to be, although, with its "stabilizer" wheels either side of its narrow, tandem two-seater body (to stop it falling over at traffic lights), it was hardly a claim that stands up.

The Monotrace was made between 1925 and 1928. Its single-cylinder, 31ci (510cc) engine was concealed in its tail, driving the rear-wheel via chains through a motorbike gearbox. Meanwhile, the driver, sitting behind a tiny windshield, steered using an enormous hybrid of a steering wheel and motorbike handlebars.

This strange design was typical of the sort of contraption French manufacturers produced before World War II, but actually hailed from Germany where it was devised by the Mauser armaments factory as the Einspur-Auto—a single-track "car". Although it had its public unveiling at the Berlin motor show in 1921, the car wasn't on sale for another two years.

On its original iteration, the stabilizer wheels were retractable, but on the Monotrace they were on outriggers that could be raised or lowered from the cockpit using a lever, and came complete with their own tiny fenders. However, what's especially intriguing in the photograph you see here is that this bizarre machine was photographed in Wales in the 1930s—in front of Bangor Hotel—with British number plates. The driver looks earnest enough, but the passenger has an expression of shyness mixed with embarrassment.

## SPECIFICATION

**YEAR REVEALED** 1925

**PLACE OF ORIGIN** St Etienne, Loire, France

**HISTORICAL STATUS** production car

**ENGINE** single-cylinder, 31ci (510cc)

**MAXIMUM POWER** unknown

**LAYOUT** rear-mounted engine driving the rear wheel

**BODYWORK** two-seater tourer

**TOP SPEED** unknown

**NUMBER BUILT** approximately 300

*"A two-wheeler manoeuvred by quite the largest steering wheel ever seen on a roadgoing vehicle."*

STEPHEN VOKINS, NATIONAL MOTOR MUSEUM, BEAULIEU, UK

The Coventry factory of Alvis in 1929; one of several manufacturers that evolved a British tradition of finely engineered sports and touring cars.

# BUGATTI TYPE 41 "ROYALE"

The 1926 Bugatti Type 41 was Ettore Bugatti's vainglorious attempt to sell his cars to emperors and kings. The lofty Italian-born carmaker called it "La Royale".

The car had a 779ci (12,763cc) straight-eight engine, with three-valves-per-cylinder, but just a single carburetor. It had a wheelbase of 14ft (4.3m), longer than a complete Subaru Impreza, and its overall length was longer than any factory-built limousine today at 21ft (6.4m). The Royale was a leviathan at over 7,000lb (3,175kg) in weight, with cast-alloy wheels measuring 24in (60cm) in diameter and an engine that was 1.4m (4.5ft) long. No matter what bodywork was fitted,

Bugatti badge

the car was magnificent. But Bugatti's timing was unfortunate. It took six years for the first car to be delivered in 1932, and during the intervening period the whole world had fallen victim to the chronic economic slump known as the "Great Depression."

Only six models were made in all, along with a prototype destroyed in 1931. Surplus Royale engines began to be used to power French railcars.

The surviving Royales became a myth-laden icon for vintage car buffs. In 1987, at one of the most celebrated collector's car auctions, Christies sold one for £5.5 million in front of 4,500 people at London's Royal Albert Hall.

## SPECIFICATION

**YEAR REVEALED** 1926

**PLACE OF ORIGIN** Molsheim, Alsace, France

**HISTORICAL STATUS** production car

**ENGINE** eight-cylinder, 779ci (12,763cc)

**MAXIMUM POWER** 300bhp

**LAYOUT** front-mounted engine driving the rear wheels

**BODYWORK** two-seater roadster, five-seater saloon, five-seater tourer

**TOP SPEED** unknown

**NUMBER BUILT** six

---

*"Even in sharp bends, the car stays exactly in line, and hardly tilts to the side."*

WF BRADLEY, *THE AUTOCAR* MAGAZINE—THE FIRST JOURNALIST TO DRIVE A ROYALE

The gargantuan hood of the Bugatti Royale is shown to best effect here, as are the gigantic alloy wheels; this is the Coupé Napoleon body.

# OPEL RAK 2 "ROCKET CAR"

The response of most carmakers to plans for a rocket-powered car would have been frosty. But Fritz von Opel was fascinated by the theories of Max Valier, inventor and author of *The Advance Into Space*, and in 1927 agreed to help him create just such a vehicle.

The Opel company's research department was assisted by rocket scientist Wilhelm Sander. They produced the "Rakentenwagen" (or RAK 1), equipped with solid fuel rockets. At Opel's Russelsheim test track in April 1928, the car reached 62mph (100kph) in just eight seconds. The car was then radically redesigned as the RAK 2, with huge wings on either side to counteract any tendency to leave the ground. It was equipped with 24 cluster-powder rockets, calculated to give 13,228lb (6,000kg) of thrust. At Berlin's Avus race track on May 23, the crowd went wild when Opel reached 148mph (238kph).

"Rocket Fritz" made headline news worldwide, amid speculation that the technology could transform world travel. The publicity worked wonders. It probably sweetened General Motors' buy-out of the Opel family's carmaking interests in 1928 –they received $66.7 million.

## SPECIFICATION

**YEAR REVEALED** 1928

**PLACE OF ORIGIN** Russelshiem, Germany

**HISTORICAL STATUS** speed record car

**ENGINE** rocket propulsion

**MAXIMUM POWER** unknown

**LAYOUT** rocket propulsion unit to the rear

**BODYWORK** single-seater racer

**TOP SPEED** 148mph (238kph)

**NUMBER BUILT** one

*"I step on the ignition pedal and the rockets roar behind me, throwing me forward. It's liberating. I step on the pedal again, then again and—it grips me like a rage—a fourth time."*

FRITZ VON OPEL, ON DRIVING THE RAK 2

With its prominent aircraft-style wings, this is the car in which "Rocket Fritz" made headlines around the world.

# BENTLEY 4.5 LITER "BLOWER"

The great Walter Owen Bentley of Bentley Motors rather disapproved of his most famous car, the 268ci (4,398cc) "Blower" Bentley. In the great tradition of steam (Bentley served his apprenticeship at the Great Northern Railway's Doncaster works), he preferred to gain power by increasing engine capacity.

"WO" had every right to be concerned, because, as he said, the Blower Bentley "proved endlessly unreliable, bringing the Bentley marque into disrepute." Even today, some enthusiasts question the reliability and efficiency of the enormous supercharger.

The idea of a Roots-type supercharger and a single SU carburetor mounted outside the bodywork came from engineering genius Amherst Villiers. Meanwhile, well-connected "Bentley Boy" Tim Birkin raised the capital to sponsor it from wealthy horse-racing patron, the Hon. Dorothy Paget.

Birkin's electrifying drive at Le Mans, in 1930, pushed the rival Mercedes team to breaking point, but at the cost of his own car. He handed victory to the unblown factory Bentley "Speed Six." The Blower's greatest hour came in the 1930 French Grand Prix, however, where it finished an amazing second—averaging over 90mph (145kph)—and very nearly won.

"The Bentley was like a large Sealyham among greyhounds," Birkin recalled in his autobiography. But the glory was shortlived. Paget withdrew her backing, Rolls-Royce absorbed Bentley, and Birkin was forced to change his allegiance to Italian machines.

## SPECIFICATION

**YEAR REVEALED** 1929

**PLACE OF ORIGIN** Cricklewood, London, UK

**HISTORICAL STATUS** production car

**ENGINE** four-cylinder, 268ci (4,398cc)

**MAXIMUM POWER** 175bhp

**LAYOUT** front-mounted engine driving the rear wheels

**BODYWORK** two-seater roadster

**TOP SPEED** 105mph (169kph)

**NUMBER BUILT** 55

*"Bond drove it hard and well and with an almost sensual pleasure."*

IAN FLEMING, *CASINO ROYALE*, IN WHICH "007" OWNS A BLOWER BENTLEY

The "Blower" Bentley, with its supercharger prominent at the front of the car, was the epitome of vintage British racers.

# 2

## 1930–1949

# SPEEDING THROUGH THE WAR YEARS

Throughout the 1930s, automobiles boomed on four distinct levels: at the bottom, "people's cars" made motoring economical and affordable enough to attract impecunious newcomers; above that, the middle classes started to aspire to brands they thought best suited their status, and the manufacturers responded with a bewildering choice of products. Cars with the "streamlined" look was one of the new "pulls."

Above this maelstrom, sports and luxury cars aimed ever higher to provide the ultimates in their fields; and, beyond that, the quest for speed saw innovation through racing car design, and some awe-inspiring attempts at capturing speed records.

World War II brought all of this to a sudden halt as manufacturing and technical know-how were channelled into the war effort in all countries. Afterwards, things would never be quite the same again, but the new era—and the technological legacy of the conflict years—brought many fresh approaches to car design, and new models that were ingenious or pulse-racing, or both.

Don't be deceived by that radiator grille—it's a fake. The Burney Streamline's engine was in its tapering tail and, regrettably, prone to overheating.

# BURNEY STREAMLINE

Sir Dennistoun Burney was a respected defense inventor during World War I. He designed what was held to be the finest British airship of all, the R100.

But airships rapidly fell from favor after the fatal crash of the later, government-sponsored R101 in 1930, which killed 48 people. Instead, Burney applied his expertise to motoring. He found backing for his Streamline Cars from his friend Stephen Courtauld, a textile magnate with an interest in technology. With "streamline" the 1930s buzzword equivalent of "digital" today, Courtauld was eager to own an airship-inspired car himself.

The fabric-covered body frame of Burney's "R100 on wheels" was built like an aircraft fuselage, a sort of inverted truss steel girder, cross-braced by strainer wires, with a completely flat underside.

Rear-engined, the Burney had all-round independent suspension, and a spare wheel was concealed inside the rear door. Seven passengers could be carried and, despite appearances, the Burney was said to handle well and 80mph touch (129kph).

A twin-cam, straight-eight engine provided the power. Yet despite being housed in a projecting case with massive air scoops, it overheated badly and was even prone to catching fire. It was also so expensive that only a few novelty crazed patrons—for that's what Burney Streamline buyers were, the Prince of Wales among them—bought one.

## SPECIFICATION

**YEAR REVEALED** 1930

**PLACE OF ORIGIN** Maidenhead, Berkshire, UK

**HISTORICAL STATUS** production car

**ENGINE** eight-cylinder, 180ci (2,956cc)

**MAXIMUM POWER** unknown

**LAYOUT** rear-mounted engine driving the rear wheels

**BODYWORK** four-door seven-seater sedan

**TOP SPEED** 80mph (129kph)

**NUMBER BUILT** 12

*"[I want] to show that a properly streamlined car would score over its more conventional competitors."* SIR DENNISTOUN BURNEY

# CITROËN PETITE ROSALIE

These days, with rigorous prototype testing and computer-aided manufacturing, we take our cars' reliability for granted. Carmakers have every confidence their products will last.

It was very different in the early 1930s, when human error meant that few cars—and roads—could be entirely depended upon. In this environment, Citroën decided to prove the longevity of its products.

Its smart new 8CV Rosalie model made its debut at the 1932 Paris motor show, with an up-to-the-minute unitary-construction body and a 89ci (1,452cc) engine, advertised as "floating power."

Citroën arrived at the Montlhéry race track in 1933 with a special 8CV. It was called "Petite Rosalie" thanks to its cut-down, skimpy two-seater body. The idea was to see how far the car could be driven, non-stop, with a team of drivers.

The car ran for 133 days and nights, and only stopped when it had covered over 186,000 miles (300,000km). This incredible total—120,000 laps at an average speed of 58mph (93kph) brought Citroën enormous publicity. Petite Rosalie also broke or established 300 other records. Before long, the name Rosalie became a byword for dependability.

## SPECIFICATION

**YEAR REVEALED** 1933

**PLACE OF ORIGIN** Paris, France

**HISTORICAL STATUS** speed record car

**ENGINE** four-cylinder, 89ci (1,452cc)

**MAXIMUM POWER** 32bhp

**LAYOUT** front-mounted engine driving the rear wheels

**BODYWORK** two-seater roadster

**TOP SPEED** 70mph (113kph)

**NUMBER BUILT** one

*"It has been said that publicity makes people buy once, but credibility makes them buy twice."*

ANDRÉ CITROËN

Citroën's "Petite Rosalie" at Montlhéry during its 133-day record run, to prove the stamina the firm put into its 8CV model.

Despite its gargantuan proportions, this Maybach Zeppelin with body designed by Paul Jaray and built by Spohn was cutting-edge stuff.

# MAYBACH DS8 ZEPPELIN

Wilhelm Maybach partnered Gottlieb Daimler in designing some of the very earliest cars, but in 1907 he went into business with Daimler's son Karl. Their speciality was building engines for Count Zeppelin's airships. After the Treaty of Versailles (which banned German companies from making aero engines), Karl turned to producing car engines. Customers proved elusive however, so in 1921, the retired Maybach built his own car.

They were acclaimed as "German Rolls-Royces." In 1928, Maybach came up with the huge and impressive DS chassis, plus a magnificent V12 engine to power it. In 1930, it was renamed the

Maybach badge

Maybach Zeppelin in honor of the pioneering aviator, just before the ultimate edition, the DS8, was launched.

To give an idea of its scale, a Ford Fiesta could park within its 12ft (3.7m) wheelbase, the engine was fronted by a radiator 3ft (90cm) wide—both residing under a 7ft- (2m-) long hood—and the gearbox was an eight-speeder. Buyers commissioned custom-made bodies from their favored coachbuilders—one car cost the same as five large homes.

Between 1921 and 1941 about 2,000 Maybachs were sold in all. The company made diesel rail engines until 1960, when it was acquired by Mercedes-Benz.

## SPECIFICATION

**YEAR REVEALED**  1931

**PLACE OF ORIGIN**
Friedrichshafen, Germany

**HISTORICAL STATUS**
production car

**ENGINE**  V12-cylinder, 487ci (7,978cc)

**MAXIMUM POWER**  200bhp

**LAYOUT**  front-mounted engine driving the rear wheels

**BODYWORK**  five- and seven-seater sedans and limousines, two-seater roadster

**TOP SPEED**  103mph (166kph)

**NUMBER BUILT**  approximately 175

*"The layman can also see that much of the resistance to the free flow of air has been avoided. Even the door handles embedded in the surfaces demonstrate this careful approach."*

MOTOR UND SPORT MAGAZINE, 1932, ON THE JARAY MAYBACH ZEPPELIN ILLUSTRATED

# CHRYSLER AIRFLOW

The Airflow today resembles a seminal example of motorized Art Deco. It was an extremely adventurous car for Chrysler but, sadly, a disaster in sales terms.

Company founder Walter Chrysler had great faith in a team of consultant engineers nicknamed the "Three Musketeers"—Carl Breer, Fred Zeder, and Owen Skelton. It was Breer's fascination with aerodynamics that led the trio to map out America's first mainstream car with this science as its guiding principle. By 1930, they had tested over 50 different experimental models in a wind tunnel constructed with input from aviation pioneer Orville Wright.

To improve ride and handling of what became the Airflow, they shifted the engine forward over the front wheels and positioned the passenger seats within the wheelbase, for better weight distribution. To cut weight they also devised a one-piece body with a lightweight metal frame (as opposed to the more common heavy, timber framing).

Early Airflows were, apparently, fraught with quality problems because of new welding techniques. But the main problem with sales was public resistance. Buyers preferred their cars to be more traditional-looking than the amorphous visage and faired-in wheels of the Airflow.

Ironically, in an attempt to boost sales, the car was actually made less aerodynamic in 1936 when a prominent trunk was added to its tapering tail but, by then, Chrysler's more traditional cars were outselling it massively. It was axed after 1937.

## SPECIFICATION

**YEAR REVEALED** 1934

**PLACE OF ORIGIN** Detroit, Michigan

**HISTORICAL STATUS** production car

**ENGINE** eight-cylinder, 298ci (4,883cc) (others up to 385ci/6,306cc)

**MAXIMUM POWER** 122bhp

**LAYOUT** front-mounted engine driving the rear wheels

**BODYWORK** two- or four-door six-seater sedan

**TOP SPEED** 88mph (142kph)

**NUMBER BUILT** 29,345

*"Research is the answer, if anyone should ask why modern cars are so much improved."*

WALTER P. CHRYSLER, WRITING IN HIS AUTOBIOGRAPHY
*LIFE OF AN AMERICAN WORKMAN*, 1937

The two-piece windshield was soon replaced by a single curved pane.

The Airflow's scientifically shaped lines were ahead of their time, and proved a bit too futuristic for the tastes of car buyers in the mid-1930s.

The location is Berlin in the 1920s, and the three cars in the foreground are to the designs of pioneering Hungarian designer Paul Jaray. They may look bizarre today but this trio, a 1922 Ley T6 at the front, a 1923 Audi Type K behind, and a 1923 Dixi G7 at the rear, had a profound influence on car design through the 1930s and beyond. As the contrast of the fourth, conventional car in the background shows, Jaray's theories led to a smoothing of the various elements of a car's bodywork.

With its entire driveline positioned ahead of the passenger compartment, the Citroën Traction Avant was a remarkably low-slung car.

# CITROËN TRACTION AVANT

Traction Avant is the French for "front-wheel drive," one of the many innovations first introduced by Citroën on this charismatic and long-running car range.

When first seen as the Citroën 7A in 1934, the four-door sedan was very modern. Its low-slung appearance came from having the entire drivetrain mounted ahead of the cabin. Engine power was through a three-speed manual gearbox in front of the engine with driveshafts to the front wheels.

The construction of the car also broke new ground, being a welded monocoque sedan that did away with a separate chassis frame altogether. Combined with the front-drive and torsion bar front suspension, the car had fantastic roadholding for its time, but was hard work to steer.

The 7A was rather underpowered with its 80ci (1,303cc) engine. Later in 1934, it was joined by the 11 Legere with a 117ci (1,911cc) motor (Light 15 in the UK, denoting the two countries' different taxation ratings for engine power). This became the signature model, although there was also a "15" six-cylinder version, and a wide choice of bodies, including sedans with a choice of two wheelbases, convertibles, and station wagons.

The Traction Avant became synonymous with egalitarian Parisian style. Yet, although there were few teething troubles, the huge investment needed to put them on sale brought Citroën to bankruptcy. The stress is said to have killed company founder André Citroën, although his company was rescued by tiremaker Michelin, a major creditor.

---

## SPECIFICATION

**YEAR REVEALED**  1934

**PLACE OF ORIGIN**  Paris, France

**HISTORICAL STATUS**
production car

**ENGINE**  four-cylinder, 80ci (1,303cc)

**MAXIMUM POWER**  32bhp

**LAYOUT**  front-mounted engine driving the front wheels

**BODYWORK**  four-door five-seater sedan

**TOP SPEED**  59mph (95kph)

**NUMBER BUILT**  88,066 (7 versions only—759,123 Traction Avants in total)

---

*"A steel greyhound and an emissary which will spread far afield the message of a new, confident France."*

L'AUTO MAGAZINE, 1934

This period "ghost" graphic shows the Citroën's novel monocoque build.

# TATRA TYPE 77

It is incredible to think that, in 1934, just about the most futuristic car in the world hailed not from Germany or the US, but from Czechoslovakia. It was the centerpiece for the proud nation's talents at the Berlin Auto Salon that year, and narrowly beat Chrysler's Airflow into production as the world's first customer-ready, scientifically-streamlined motor car.

The car came about thanks to the personal vision of Tatra's widely admired Austrian chief engineer Hans Ledwinka. It brought together his expertise in air-cooled engines and intelligent chassis design, with a newfound enthusiasm for aerodynamics.

At its core was a welded box-section chassis, a sort of metal backbone with a forked extension at the back to cradle the air-cooled, overhead-camshaft V8 engine designed specially for this car. The entire powerpack, gearbox included, could be easily unbolted and detached for repairs.

With the mechanical elements at the rear, Ledwinka could concentrate on the T77's excellent streamlining—the first in a long line of luxury Czech cars. It had a small frontal area, a windshield angled at 45 degrees, and carefully sculpted air intakes on the body sides and on the long, tapering tail, to cool the engine as it drove along. The later T77A, with a bigger engine, five seats instead of six, and a steering wheel on the right instead of the original central steering position, was given a centrally positioned tailfin to aid high-speed stability—a highly distinctive feature.

## SPECIFICATION

**YEAR REVEALED**  1934

**PLACE OF ORIGIN**  Koprivnice, Czechoslovakia

**HISTORICAL STATUS**
production car

**ENGINE**  V8-cylinder, 181–206ci (2,968–3,377cc)

**MAXIMUM POWER**  73bhp

**LAYOUT**  rear-mounted engine driving the rear wheels

**BODYWORK**  four-door five-seater sedan

**TOP SPEED**  93mph (150kph)

**NUMBER BUILT**  255

*"A design of great interest embodying in principle the ideals of many designers."*  THE AUTOCAR MAGAZINE, 1935

The Tatra 77 was a masterpiece of design and science in 1934, with its careful attention to streamlining detail and powerful V8 engine.

The appreciative crowd give an idea of the scale of the 1935 incarnation of Bluebird, which would set the world land speed record.

# BLUEBIRD

Bluebird was not one single vehicle but a long series of cars and motor boats used to challenge world speed records. The 350bhp Sunbeam (see pages 46–47)was just one of the early models.

Bluebird was the "lucky" name of Sir Malcolm Campbell (and later of his record-breaking son, Donald), the descendant of a wealthy London diamond-dealing family who began his car-racing exploits in 1910.

Having topped 150mph (241kph) in the Sunbeam, he now set his sights on bettering 200mph (322kph), which he achieved in 1928 using, for the first time, a car designed to his precise requirements. At its heart was a 450bhp Napier Lion 12-cylinder aero engine. Constantly updated and modified, by 1931 Bluebird featured a supercharged, 950bhp Napier V12 engine. Campbell took the record to 246.09mph (396.04kph), and was knighted for his heroic feat. But there was no stopping him. In 1932, he became the first man on earth past 250mph (402kph).

The car pictured here was crafted in partnership with engineer Reid Railton in 1935, with power coming from a huge 2,232ci (36,582cc) supercharged Rolls-Royce R-type V12 aero engine. The design of this unit, at the time, was a closely guarded secret, but Rolls was eager to share the huge publicity Campbell generated. Thoroughly developed from earlier Bluebirds, it now had full-width bodywork and twin rear wheels. Driving it on the Bonneville Salt Flats in Utah, he achieved an amazing, record-beating 301.129mph (484.620kph).

## SPECIFICATION

**YEAR REVEALED** 1935

**PLACE OF ORIGIN** Brooklands, Surrey, UK

**HISTORICAL STATUS** speed record car

**ENGINE** V12-cylinder, 2,232ci (36,582cc)

**MAXIMUM POWER** 2,500bhp

**LAYOUT** rear-mounted engine driving the rear wheels

**BODYWORK** single-seater racer

**TOP SPEED** 301mph (484kph)

**NUMBER BUILT** one

*"Salt is the ideal surface for tired LSR cars because it gives far better grip than tarmac. But he [Campbell] wasn't to have an easy time. On the first of his two-way runs, a tire burst at 304mph."*

RICHARD NOBLE, FORMER WORLD LAND SPEED RECORD HOLDER, WRITING IN *AUTOCAR* MAGAZINE, 1996

# STOUT SCARAB

The earliest thinking behind the MPV (multi-purpose vehicle or multi-passenger vehicle) format as we recognize today can be traced back to 1935 and William Bushnell Stout's Scarab.

This Detroit entrepreneur and inventor took his inspiration from airplanes. With his experience of designing an all-metal twin-engined aircraft, he decided to adapt the fuselage into a vehicle intended to be an office-on-wheels.

To make maximium use of space "on board," he placed the engine, a Ford V8, at the very back, and moved the driving position forward so the steering wheel was almost directly above the front wheels. There was no "hood" to speak of. The wheels were positioned at each corner and the streamlined profile had what car designers today call a "monospace" (or "one-box") shape—with no visually separated engine or luggage compartments.

Although the driver's seat was fixed into position, the rear bench seat had cushions that could be rearranged into a full-length bed, the front passenger seat could swivel round to face the rear, and a fold-down table was hinged on the left side of the interior for meetings. However, at a cost of $5,000 each, just nine were sold.

## SPECIFICATION

**YEAR REVEALED** 1935

**PLACE OF ORIGIN** Dearborn, Michigan

**HISTORICAL STATUS** semi-production car

**ENGINE** V8-cylinder, 221ci (3,622cc)

**MAXIMUM POWER** 85bhp

**LAYOUT** rear-mounted engine driving the rear wheels

**BODYWORK** three-door five-seater sedan

**TOP SPEED** unknown

**NUMBER BUILT** nine

*"In 1935, Stout rocked the automobile industry with the sensation caused by his Scarab car. Its appearance was so startling that people would ask, 'Which way is it going?'"*

ODERN MECHANIX MAGAZINE, 1943

William Stout's Scarab was a fascinating forerunner to today's omnipresent multi-purpose vehicle.

The Auto Union Type-C was a key element of Germany's quest for motor sport dominance—tricky to drive, yet fearsomely capable.

# AUTO UNION TYPE-C

After losing his job as technical director of German carmaker Steyr in 1930, the renowned Dr. Ferdinand Porsche finally decided to open his own car engineering consultancy. His timing was unfortunate because the world was reeling from economic recession, but between commissions, Porsche and his chief designer Karl Rabe weren't idle. They decided to design the ultimate racing car engine, a 262ci (4,300cc) V16 with two cylinder blocks angled at 45 degrees and 32 valves, despite having no client for it.

The Auto Union company was created in 1932 by the merger of Audi, DKW, Horch and Wanderer, and this new organization decided to promote itself through Grand Prix racing. The newly installed German chancellor, Adolf Hitler, pledged to back the venture, and Porsche was contracted to design the new car to go with his existing engine for the 1934 season.

The car was mid-engined with all-independent suspension and a fuel tank located between driver and engine. The layout anticipated the prevalent Grand Prix format by over 25 years.

The Type-C was the third and most powerful evolution of the Auto Union racing car. Its supercharged V16 was now 367ci (6,006cc), and former handling problems were addressed with a ZF limited-slip differential.

The car won 6 of the 12 races that season and Bernd Rosemeyer (killed in a stream-lined Type-C during a 1938 record assault) was crowned European champion. In fact, the Type-C won 33 victories from 59 races.

## SPECIFICATION

**YEAR REVEALED** 1935

**PLACE OF ORIGIN** Zwickau, Germany

**HISTORICAL STATUS** Grand Prix racing car

**ENGINE** V16-cylinder, 367ci (6,006cc)

**MAXIMUM POWER** 520bhp

**LAYOUT** mid-mounted engine driving the rear wheels

**BODYWORK** single-seater racer

**TOP SPEED** 211mph (340kph)

**NUMBER BUILT** 30 different cars raced, but some were evolutions rather than completely new models

*"My dream of getting behind the wheel of this car has come true and I am fully aware of how privileged I am to do so."*

NICK MASON, PINK FLOYD MUSICIAN, AFTER DRIVING A SURVIVING TYPE-C IN 2007

# PEUGEOT 402 ANDREAU "1940"

It was extremely unusual for car manufacturers to exhibit "concept" or show cars in the 1930s, so the appearance of this astonishing looking Peugeot four-door sedan at the 1936 Paris Salon caused a stir.

It was presented as a vision of the family sedan of the near-future—1940 was the target—a risky strategy since it implied that the year-old sedan from which it was derived might soon be obsolete.

The 402 sedan itself was a sleek-looking car, with gracefully curved fenders, and headlamps concealed behind a waterfall-style radiator grille. But it wasn't very aerodynamic. The "theoretical model" had wind-cheating science applied to it by Jean Andreau, an eminent consultant from the Conservatoire Nationale des Arts et Metiers.

The large tailfin was an obvious benefit, but the barrel profile of the sides, lack of running boards, rear-wheel fairings, and the stunningly curvaceous windshield were all integral to the design. The streamlined shape meant that the car's top speed, at 87mph (140kph), was 16mph (26kph) more than a standard 402 with identical engine.

The car became the first of six research prototypes for future Peugeots. The one shown here, codenamed N4X and the sole survivor, features a simply stunning panoramic windshield merging into the door glass, which would have given unparalleled visibility to the driver. But events overtook Peugeot's plans: the entire project was abandoned as the dark clouds of World War II gathered.

## SPECIFICATION

**YEAR REVEALED** 1936

**PLACE OF ORIGIN** Paris, France

**HISTORICAL STATUS** prototype

**ENGINE** four-cylinder, 121ci (1,991cc)

**MAXIMUM POWER** 55bhp

**LAYOUT** front-mounted engine driving the rear wheels

**BODYWORK** four-door five-seater sedan

**TOP SPEED** 87mph (140kph)

**NUMBER BUILT** six

*"Reduction in vertical lift is important in achieving equilibrium at high speeds, by stabilizing the vehicle through shifting the center of lateral thrust rearward."*

FROM A PEUGEOT PRESS RELEASE, 1936

N4X, one of six experimental Peugeots built to test the limits of streamlining for family cars in the near future—which, then, was the 1940s.

A Toyota AB, the convertible version of the AA model that was to lay the foundation stone for Toyota's success.

# TOYOTA AA

Japanese giant Toyota had an unsteady introduction to the car world. The company specialized in making textile looms until 1935, when a windfall on the sale of some patents persuaded Kiichiro Toyoda, son of the founder, to consider entering the car business.

It was no surprise that the three prototypes he built in May 1935 bore an uncanny resemblance to the Chrysler Airflow—the Toyoda Automatic Loom Works had bought one to take apart, and closely modeled the A-1 on it. They used Toyoda's newly designed Type A six-cylinder engine in a ladder-type chassis, closely copied from Ford. Yet, unusually for the time, it had pressed-steel disc wheels and a curved, one-piece windshield.

Toyoda suspended its fledgling car project to concentrate on the G1 truck, considered a more profitable venture. In 1937, however, the car was finally announced for sale under the name Toyota AA.

Why the change? In July 1937, Kiichiro held a competition to find a new logo for the firm's vehicle-making venture. The winner, from over 20,000 entries, suggested a harmonious shape in which the Japanese characters suggested speed but, because it used only eight brushstrokes, it was also deemed a symbol of burgeoning prosperity. It was made to align phonetically with the company name by changing the word from "Toyoda" to "Toyota"; Kiichiro also liked the distance it put between the car and its family business origins.

## SPECIFICATION

**YEAR REVEALED** 1937

**PLACE OF ORIGIN** Koromo City, Japan

**HISTORICAL STATUS** production car

**ENGINE** six-cylinder, 207ci (3,389cc)

**MAXIMUM POWER** 62bhp

**LAYOUT** front-mounted engine driving the rear wheels

**BODYWORK** four-door five-seater sedan

**TOP SPEED** unknown

**NUMBER BUILT** 1,404

*"We must all exert whatever efforts are necessary to build the kind of cars which will win out in competition with the products produced by overseas companies."*

KIICHIRO TOYODA

The unique Fiat speed car created by Raffaele Cecchini had its engine capacity reduced to chase 31ci (500cc) records.

# FIAT 500 TIPO CORSA

Even when Fiat tackled the low-price end of the car scale, it was incapable of building anything that didn't exude character, verve, and speed "potential."

Italian printer and amateur racing driver Raffaele Cecchini, however, went further than most, to wring maximum performance from the Fiat 500, the 1936 car Italians nicknamed "Il Topolino" (little mouse). In 1938, he created this little streamliner to chase a number of 31ci (500cc) class speed records at the Monza circuit.

Apart from the beaten aluminum torpedo-like bodywork, with its gaping air intake, incredible fish tail, disc wheels, and tiny off-set turret, the usually feeble Topolino engine was heavily modified. To ensure it met 31ci (500cc) class rules (the standard Topolino had a 35ci (569cc) engine, sleeves were fitted inside the cylinder, and a new crankshaft gave a shorter stroke to reduce capacity to 30.45ci (499.05cc). Power output was boosted using a Cozette carburetor and supercharger, the side valves replaced with a Siata overhead-valve conversion, and the car was cooled with a front-mounted radiator. Considering the basic Fiat could manage just 53mph (85kph), Cecchini worked wonders turning it into a 90mph (145kph) catapult.

At Monza, the driver set record speeds for 50-, 100-, and 200-mile (80-, 161-, and 322-km) stints at 85.39mph (137.42kph), 86.18mph (138.69kph), and 81.97mph (131.92kph) respectively. Not bad for a car originally intended as a city runabout.

## SPECIFICATION

**YEAR REVEALED** 1938

**PLACE OF ORIGIN** Turin, Italy

**HISTORICAL STATUS** production car-based single-seater speed record car

**ENGINE** four-cylinder, 30.45ci (499.05cc)

**MAXIMUM POWER** unknown

**LAYOUT** front-mounted engine driving the rear wheels

**BODYWORK** one-door, single-seater sedan

**TOP SPEED** 90mph (145kph)

**NUMBER BUILT** one

*"Do not be misled by the conning tower, which suggests that the driver's head is enclosed; there is a gap between the front and rear portions, as Cecchini has to breathe like the rest of us."*

"THE BLOWER," WRITING IN *THE LIGHT CAR* MAGAZINE, JUNE 1938

The Fiat 500 was nicknamed "Topolino" by an adoring Italian public.

# CHRYSLER THUNDERBOLT

Even today, there's something irresistibly futuristic about the Chrysler Thunderbolt. It's also extremely evocative, its pontoon-like body having been the inspiration for millions of tin toy cars of the 1940–50s.

Six Thunderbolts were created for a nationwide tour of American Chrysler dealers, intended to add spice to the introduction of the 1941 model-year Chrysler cars in showrooms across the country. The name came from a car that had smashed the land speed record at Bonneville Salt Flats, Utah, in 1938. Each car had a chrome lightning flash on its doors.

The basis for the cars was the chassis of the straight-eight Chrysler New Yorker, but the novel bodies were built by the Briggs coachwork firm to the design of Alex Tremulis, a leading independent stylist of the time.

The pontoon-like profile was shocking enough at the time, with slab sides completely enclosing the wheels. But within this aluminum outer skin were other innovations, including an electrically retractable hardtop and headlights, doors that opened via discreet push buttons, and the novel idea of an air intake under the front bumper.

## SPECIFICATION

**YEAR REVEALED** 1941

**PLACE OF ORIGIN** Detroit, Michigan

**HISTORICAL STATUS** prototype

**ENGINE** eight-cylinder, 323ci (5,301cc)

**MAXIMUM POWER** 143bhp

**LAYOUT** front-mounted engine driving the rear wheels

**BODYWORK** two-door two-seater roadster

**TOP SPEED** unknown

**NUMBER BUILT** six

*"His fertile imagination was clearly geared to space-age images, and it aligned him with much of the thinking in post-war car design."*

PROFESSOR PENNY SPARKE, DESIGN HISTORIAN, ON ALEX TREMULIS

Thunderbolts toured Chrysler's North American dealers to promote the 1941 range.

With the driver in the snug, single-seater cockpit, this picture gives a clear idea of the immense scale of the **T80** and its incredible contours.

# MERCEDES-BENZ T80

This car is the ultimate manifestation of speed as envisioned at the height of Nazi power in Germany.

The monstrous six-wheeler was a pet project of racing driver Hans Stuck, who wanted Germany to assert its engineering supremacy by grabbing the world land speed record. Stuck had the ear of Adolf Hitler, who eagerly gave the venture state backing. The dream team of constructor Mercedes-Benz and designer Ferdinand Porsche were, by 1937, hard at work on what became the T80.

At the heart of the six-wheeler chassis was a vast 2,716ci (44,500cc) V12 engine—a Mercedes aero engine more usually found in the Messerschmitt Bf 109 fighter plane. Only, in this incarnation, power was doubled to a projected 3,000bhp, using a fuel mixture of mostly alcohol. The four rear wheels were all driven using a "slipping clutch" system, instead of a gearbox, to match them to engine power at 93mph (150kph).

The steel spaceframe, meanwhile, was covered in a startling, winged body, complete with faired-in cockpit, and achieved an incredible drag coefficient of just 0.18.

During the design process, the target speed rose from 342 to 373mph (550 to 600kph), and ultimately to 435mph (700kph), as the record was pushed higher by British rivals George Eyston and John Cobb. Test runs in October 1939 revealed that the T80 needed more development work. The record run was postponed, permanently, by the onset of war.

## SPECIFICATION

**YEAR REVEALED** 1939

**PLACE OF ORIGIN** Stuttgart, Germany

**HISTORICAL STATUS** speed record car

**ENGINE** V12-cylinder, 2,716ci (44,500cc)

**MAXIMUM POWER** 3,000bhp (estimated)

**LAYOUT** mid-mounted engine driving the rear wheels

**BODYWORK** single-seater racer

**TOP SPEED** 373mph (600kph)

**NUMBER BUILT** one

*"In order to bring the car to a stop after just 1km of braking distance, as calculated by Porsche, the T80 was fitted with six brake drums each 500mm in diameter."*

FROM *PORSCHE SPECIALS* BY LOTHAR BOSCHEN & JURGEN BARTH, 1986

Laid bare, the T80 reveals its six wheels and 2,716ci (44,500cc) fighter plane engine.

# KDF-WAGEN/VOLKSWAGEN

The beginnings of the best-selling single car design ever—21,529,464 were bought by the time manufacture ended in 2003—go further back than September 1939, when the car in its final form was revealed.

The German "people's car" (volkswagen) project was first announced at the Berlin motor show in 1934, after the Nazi government-backed German Automobile Industry Association officially engaged the Porsche design consultancy to create it.

Ferdinand Porsche drew on designs for rear-engined economy cars he'd undertaken for Zundapp and NSU (denying accusations of intellectual theft from Czechoslovakia's Tatra). These featured semi-trailing arm suspension and an air-cooled, flat-four engine mounted in the tail of the vehicle.

In 1937, following close collaboration with the German government on the design parameters, a batch of 30 prototypes, built by Mercedes-Benz, began 1.8 million miles (2.9 million km) of testing on Black Forest country roads and the new autobahns. In 1938, the production plant, 50 miles (80km) east of Hanover, was inaugurated, and a Government-scheme called "Kraft durch Freude" (Strength Through Joy) offered attractive subscription terms for a new Volkswagen. It attracted 336,000 "savers," none of whom ultimately received their cars. No sooner had the Volkswagen been revealed, Germany was at war and the factory was used to make military vehicles. It was heavily bombed in 1944, but reconstructed by Allied Forces in 1945.

## SPECIFICATION

**YEAR REVEALED** 1939

**PLACE OF ORIGIN** Hanover, Germany

**HISTORICAL STATUS** production-ready car

**ENGINE** four-cylinder, 60ci (984cc)

**MAXIMUM POWER** 24bhp

**LAYOUT** rear-mounted engine driving the rear wheels

**BODYWORK** two-door four-seater saloon

**TOP SPEED** 62mph (100kph)

**NUMBER BUILT** 630 to 1,944 (none sold to the public)

*"It is too ugly and too noisy. To build the car commercially would be a completely uneconomic enterprise."*

FROM A REPORT ON VOLKSWAGEN BY A BRITISH MOTOR INDUSTRY DELEGATION, 1946

A 1949 Volkswagen, the definitive production form of what became known as the Beetle.

This evocative painting depicts the three VW prototypes that hit the road in fall 1936, under the attentive eye of the Nazi regime.

GIs test an early Jeep at Fort Sam Houston, Texas, in 1941, seeing how it would—literally—fly over tough terrain.

# WILLYS MB JEEP

In 1938, with war clouds gathering over Europe, the US Army decided to replace its motorized motorcycle-sidecar combinations (used for messenger and advance reconnaissance duties) with a small, general-purpose vehicle. It let American motor manufacturers know its requirements in 1940, and three companies responded with prototype vehicles—Willys Overland's Quad, the American Bantam Car Co.'s Blitz Buggy, and the Ford Motor Company's GP.

After a protracted and complex bidding process, Willys's concept for a light 2,106lb (955kg), maneuverable, and powerful all-purpose vehicle, capable of carrying troops as well as weapons, was selected for production. It boasted selectable two- or four-wheel drive—a true breakthrough.

It went on to serve in every major World War II campaign as a machine-gun firing mount, reconnaissance vehicle, pick-up truck, frontline limousine, ammunition bearer, wire-layer, and taxi. In the Ardennes during the 1944–45 Battle of the Bulge, Jeeps loaded with stretchers, raced to safety ahead of spearheading Nazi armor. In Egypt, Britain used a combat patrol of Jeeps to knock out a fleet of fuel tankers en route to German Field Marshal Rommel's armour forces on the eve of the battle of El Alamein.

"Jeep" soon became a household word, many assuming it was a slurring of the acronym GP, for General Purpose. Willys offered civilian editions from 1945, and the Jeep name was registered as an international trademark five years later.

## SPECIFICATION

**YEAR REVEALED**  1942

**PLACE OF ORIGIN**  Toledo, Ohio

**HISTORICAL STATUS** production car

**ENGINE**  four-cylinder, 134ci (2,199cc)

**MAXIMUM POWER**  60bhp

**LAYOUT**  front-mounted engine driving all four wheels

**BODYWORK**  four-seater utility

**TOP SPEED**  60mph (97kph)

**NUMBER BUILT**  363,000 (plus 280,000 made by licensee Ford, and 2,675 by Bantam)

*"America's greatest contribution to modern warfare."*  GENERAL GEORGE C. MARSHALL, ON WILLYS MB JEEP

The Willys Jeep was a battlefield legend in World War II.

# HEALEY 2.4-LITER

With gas strictly rationed, and most new cars earmarked for export, motoring was difficult in 1940s Britain. So when news broke that Donald Healey's sporty new 146ci (2,400cc) had recorded a best speed of 111mph (179kph) on the Jabbeke Highway in Belgium in 1947, it was especially uplifting news. Here was something Britain could be proud of: the world's fastest production sedan and, hopefully, a taste of good times to come.

Donald Healey, exuberant pre-war rally driver and Triumph technical director, had come up with a totally new car. Its light, but rigid cruciform-braced chassis featured advanced front trailing link suspension and was powered by an excellent Riley twin-camshaft, twin-carburetor engine.

Initially there were two models: the open Westland and Elliot sedan, both with hallmark kite-shaped grilles and bodies in "Birmabright" aluminum over an ash wood frame. Healey and other contemporary drivers campaigned the cars with panache in great events, such as Italy's Mille Miglia, in which one won the Touring Car class in 1948.

Healeys didn't come cheap. The £2,725 luxurious Elliott, inflated by double Purchase Tax because the basic car cost over £1,000 (actually £1,750), put it beyond the reach of all but a few. There were later variations on the original 146ci (2,400cc) cars, but after rights to the Healey 100 were sold to the British Motor Corporation in 1952 (becoming the Austin-Healey 100/4), Healey as a separate marque was wound up.

## SPECIFICATION

**YEAR REVEALED** 1946

**PLACE OF ORIGIN** Warwick, Warwickshire, UK

**HISTORICAL STATUS** production car

**ENGINE** four-cylinder, 146ci (2,400cc)

**MAXIMUM POWER** 101bhp

**LAYOUT** front-mounted engine driving the rear wheels

**BODYWORK** two-door Elliot four-seater saloon or Westland tourer

**TOP SPEED** 111mph (179kph)

**NUMBER BUILT** 165

*"If we want to sell to America, we don't send the sales manager because we don't have one. I just send myself."*

DONALD HEALEY, *THE AUTOCAR* MAGAZINE, MAY 1948

A standard 146ci 2, (400cc) sedan like this touched 111mph (179kph) in a demonstration run.

The diminutive figure of Donald Healey at the wheel of an early Healey 2.4; with the flip-up headlight covers not featured on production versions.

A genuine "flying car" was up, up, and away in November 1947, when Consolidated-Vultee's ConvAircar Model 116 took off and circled San Diego, California, for over an hour. The plastic-bodied car had a clip-on Lycoming wing/engine unit, so the lightweight four-seater could be driven away from airstrips.

Preston Tucker stands proudly by his creation, the ill-starred 48; its advanced features included a rear-mounted engine and a padded dashboard.

# TUCKER 48 "TORPEDO"

Preston T. Tucker's character was something between dreamer and opportunist. He'd been an office boy at Cadillac, a car salesman, and partner in an Indianapolis racing car business before deciding to revolutionize car design in post-war America with an all-new model that was fast, stylish, and safe.

Early ideas in 1945 were for a streamlined coupé with a rear-mounted, 592ci (9,700cc), air-cooled engine that used two torque converters to the rear wheels instead of a gearbox. It had seatbelts, a padded dashboard, and a windshield that popped out in a crash. When that proved unfeasible, his team went for a streamlined four-door sedan, with a Franklin air-cooled flat-six engine in the back. The seatbelts were dropped, because it was felt they implied the car was unsafe, and so were swiveling headlamps, disc brakes, and a central driving position. But the independent suspension and padded dashboard remained. The car's ongoing evolution meant a switch to water-cooling, and the finalized version proved rapid, with a 121mph (195kph) top speed despite its considerable bulk.

In 1946, Tucker acquired the then largest factory building in the world, a former Chicago aircraft plant, to make his car. But public goodwill evaporated when US financial regulators alleged fraud for raising finance from dealers and customers while changing the design of the car they had committed to. His name was cleared, but the Tucker Corporation went into liquidation.

## SPECIFICATION

**YEAR REVEALED**  1947

**PLACE OF ORIGIN**  Chicago, Illinois

**HISTORICAL STATUS**  production car

**ENGINE**  flat six-cylinder, 335ci (5,491cc)

**MAXIMUM POWER**  166bhp

**LAYOUT**  rear-mounted engine driving the rear wheels

**BODYWORK**  four-door five-seater sedan

**TOP SPEED**  121mph (195kph)

**NUMBER BUILT**  51

*"Millions of dollars of the taxpayers' money have been squandered in an utterly fruitless effort to kill the Tucker."*

PRESTON TUCKER IN *AN OPEN LETTER TO THE AUTOMOBILE INDUSTRY*, 1948

# CISITALIA 202

Most people have never heard of Cisitalia but, without the landmark Pininfarina design for the elfin 202 coupé, today's cars would look very different.

It was the first "modern" looking GT car to establish leading Italian stylists. Its hood was lower than its front wings; its headlights blended into the body rather than being freestanding; and its unadorned, low-slung profile broke away from the bulky, traditional look that cars still retained.

Its wings, for instance, were totally integrated into the bodywork rather than suggesting old-fashioned fenders, but its overall shape was utterly harmonious. Critics soon recognized its masterpiece status. The New York Museum of Modern Art has, since 1951, kept a 202 in its permanent collection.

Cisitalia was founded in 1946 by racing driver, businessman, and one-time soccer player Piero Dusio. Calling on the services of Fiat engineer Dante Giacosa, the company's first project was a single-seater racing car with Fiat front suspension and engine.

This was followed in 1948 by the 202, using essentially the same mechanical package and tubular spaceframe under that Pininfarina-designed and built body. Thanks to extremely slippery aerodynamics, the Cisitalia topped 100mph (161kph) on just 55bhp from the tuned 66ci (1,089cc) engine.

But it wasn't to last. In 1949, Cisitalia faced bankruptcy due to over-ambitious plans for a Porsche-designed Grand Prix car. Dusio decamped to Argentina, but the 202 continued in production until 1952.

## SPECIFICATION

**YEAR REVEALED** 1947

**PLACE OF ORIGIN** Turin, Italy

**HISTORICAL STATUS** production car

**ENGINE** four-cylinder, 66ci (1,089cc)

**MAXIMUM POWER** 55bhp

**LAYOUT** front-mounted engine driving the rear wheels

**BODYWORK** two-door two-seater coupé

**TOP SPEED** 105mph (169kph)

**NUMBER BUILT** 170 (estimated)

*"Cars are rolling sculpture."*

ARTHUR DREXLER, CURATOR OF THE "EIGHT AUTOMOBILES" EXHIBITION
AT THE MUSUEM OF MODERN ART, WHICH INCLUDED THE CISITALIA 202

Cisitalia's beautiful 202 Coupé, with Pininfarina body, displayed at New York's Museum of Modern Art, where an example is permanently housed.

A removable hardtop would have been standard equipment on the four-abreast, three-wheeler Divan, had Gary Davis's ambitious plans succeeded.

# DAVIS DIVAN

The story of this arresting-looking three-wheeler with its four-abreast seating begins in 1938, when a similar one-off car was commissioned by wealthy American playboy Joel Thorne. He regularly cruised the streets of Los Angeles in his three-wheeled wonder "Californian." One man who was particularly taken with it was car salesman Glenn Gordon "Gary" Davis.

Somehow, Davis managed to acquire the car, which had inspired him to try and sell a version to American motorists. Treating the Californian as his rolling billboard and prototype, Davis toured the nation promoting his Davis Motor Car Company. Having acquired a factory in Van Nuys, and with the Californian beginning to look rather worn, Davis hired some engineers to help

him build a production prototype. Three experimental cars later, the specification of the Davis Divan was settled. It now included a 159ci (2,600cc) Hercules engine and a three-speed Borg Warner gearbox. The hardtop was removable and headlights were concealed behind flaps.

Although eye-catching, only a few were test-built before Davis's exasperated staff sued him for unpaid wages. Despite plans for making 50 cars daily and new designs for a three-wheeled military vehicle, the plant was shut in mid-1948. Davis was jailed for two years for defrauding investors; after he served his sentence in 1953, he became involved in making bumper cars. Whether or not Gary Davis was a conman, he certainly created a car like nothing else on the road.

## SPECIFICATION

**YEAR REVEALED**  1947

**PLACE OF ORIGIN**  Van Nuys, California

**HISTORICAL STATUS**
production car

**ENGINE**  four-cylinder, 159ci 2, (600cc)

**MAXIMUM POWER**  63bhp

**LAYOUT**  front-mounted engine driving the rear wheels

**BODYWORK**  two-door four-seater coupé

**TOP SPEED**  65mph (105kph) (estimated)

**NUMBER BUILT**  13

*"As peculiar as the Divan might appear, its composed road manners hint that with a bit less boasting and a lot more funding, there may have been room on American roads for this idiosyncratic three-wheeler."*    AUTOWEEK MAGAZINE, 2007

# CITROËN 2CV

At the Paris motor show in October 1948, the 2CV caused astonishment, even though it had been scheduled to appear eight years earlier. The original launch was cancelled when World War II broke out. All but one of the 250 prototypes were destroyed to preserve the ingenious car's secrets.

It expressed a new philosophy for Citroën, being the lightest of lightweight economy cars, powered by a newly designed air-cooled flat-twin engine of a mere 23ci (375cc), front-wheel drive, and the first four-speed gearbox Citroën had ever fitted as standard. Its corrugated hood gave the appearance of a wartime air-raid shelter on wheels.

The "father" of the 2CV was Citroën's managing director, Pierre Boulanger. He briefed his chief engineer Maurice Broglie to come up with an "umbrella on wheels" that could travel in comfort over rural roads and cost a third of the price of a family sedan.

The tight-knit team that designed the car, led by André Lefebvre, more than rose to the challenge, and continued work on the car during the war. After several concepts had been tried out, using a test track built in the grounds of an isolated chateau outside Paris, Citroën settled on a light, gauge steel body and soft, long-travel interconnected suspension featuring horizontal coil springs. Low-pressure Michelin Pilote tires made sure it could float over any pothole.

Showgoers in 1948 might have been uncertain as to the utilitarian new Citroën, but it rapidly became part of the fabric of French life, both rural and urban.

## SPECIFICATION

**YEAR REVEALED**  1948

**PLACE OF ORIGIN**  Paris, France

**HISTORICAL STATUS**
production car

**ENGINE**  flat twin-cylinder, 23ci (375cc)

**MAXIMUM POWER**  9bhp

**LAYOUT**  front-mounted engine
driving the front wheels

**BODYWORK**  four-door
four-seater sedan

**TOP SPEED**  40mph (64kph)

**NUMBER BUILT**  3,868,634

*"Design me a car to carry two people and 50 kilos of potatoes at 60kph, using no more than 3 liters of fuel per 100km… Let it be disgustingly economical."*

PIERRE BOULANGER, CITROËN MANAGING DIRECTOR, 1935 & 1947

These 2CV prototypes were discovered in 1994 after 55 years hidden in a barn.

The charm and meagre running costs of the 2CV helped Citroën motorize the French nation; the corrugated hood was "normalised" from 1961.

# HUDSON COMMODORE

Hudson, founded in 1909, was among the last of the American "independents"—carmakers who struggled and ultimately failed in the face of the mighty Ford, General Motors, and Chrysler. Although its cars during the 1920–30s were mostly unremarkable, Hudson shocked the burghers of Detroit in 1948 with its range of "Step Down" cars.

They were so-nicknamed because driver and passengers stepped down into their seats due to a unitary-construction method Hudson called "Monobilt": instead of the body being bolted on top of the chassis, the floorpan was suspended from the bottom of it. All the occupants sat within the chassis sidemembers, which acted as a strong, encircling perimeter frame. As part of the design, the chassis extended around the outside of the rear wheels.

Hudson's stylists then came up with sleek and handsome bodywork that made a 1948 Hudson the "car to own." The range went from the budget-priced Pacemaker to the Commodore.

Yet the firm's sales and fortunes were on the slide under ferocious pressure from the Detroit majors. In 1954, Hudson was forced to merge with Nash to survive.

## SPECIFICATION

**YEAR REVEALED**  1948

**PLACE OF ORIGIN**  Detroit, Michigan

**HISTORICAL STATUS**
production car

**ENGINE**  six-cylinder, 262ci (4,295cc) & eight-cylinder, 254ci (4,164cc)

**MAXIMUM POWER**  121bhp (six-cylinder) & 128bhp (eight-cylinder)

**LAYOUT**  front-mounted engine driving the front wheels

**BODYWORK**  six-seater saloon

**TOP SPEED**  93mph (150kph)

**NUMBER BUILT**  529,590

*"The motor car that is thrilling proof of what designers the world over have always known—that the lower a car can be built, the more graceful its lines can be made."*

FROM A HUDSON ADVERTISEMENT, 1949

The Commodore was visually almost identical to the Hornet model shown here, part of a range of "Step Down" cars.

# JAGUAR XK120

Although the XK120 was the fastest, most exotic car that Britain offered in 1948, it came about almost by accident.

In 1945, Jaguar Cars offered a range of stylish sedans and tourers, but used bought-in engines. Company founder William Lyons planned a new sedan with a brand new Jaguar-made engine, designed in secret during World War II.

This twin camshaft straight-six was a masterpiece. Flexible and powerful, its basis was a cast-iron block with a seven-bearing crankshaft. On top was an all-alloy crossflow Weslake cylinder head. It had two noise-reducing timing chains, and twin 1.75in (4.5cm) SU carburetors. It looked superb with its polished aluminum cam covers, and stove-enameled exhaust manifold.

Delays in the sedan's development meant that Jaguar had no car in which to install its showpiece. So William Lyons hastily constructed a sports car body on a shortened sedan chassis, thinking it might generate publicity and act as a rolling testbed.

The result of this was breathtaking: the XK120 was beautifully, classically proportioned and confirmed Lyons' genius as a stylist. It was fast, too. On a motorway at Jabbeke in Belgium, test driver Ron Sutton achieved 126.5mph (203.5kph), and over 132mph (212kph) with the windshield and hood removed.

Jaguar was deluged with orders, but a new problem arose: satisfying demand. Indeed, most production was exported to the US; one rarely saw an XK120 on British roads.

## SPECIFICATION

**YEAR REVEALED** 1948

**PLACE OF ORIGIN** Coventry, Warwickshire, UK

**HISTORICAL STATUS** production car

**ENGINE** six-cylinder, 209ci (3,442cc)

**MAXIMUM POWER** 160bhp

**LAYOUT** front-mounted engine driving the rear wheels

**BODYWORK** two-door two-seater roadster and coupé

**TOP SPEED** 124mph (200kph)

**NUMBER BUILT** 12,055

*"It felt comfortable in the wet and, with the Jag, it was an advantage because it lightened the steering and saved the brakes. I took the lead on the second lap and won."*

BRITISH RACING DRIVER, STIRLING MOSS, WHO WON THE
1950 TOURIST TROPHY RACE IN AN XK120, AGED 21

The gorgeous purity of the XK120's lines barely hint at the car's original purpose—it was meant to showcase Jaguar's six-cylinder XK engine.

With the addition of a boxy station wagon body, the Land Rover became a proper "car." The Defender—a direct descendant—is on sale today.

# LAND ROVER SERIES I

In the grim environment of post-war Britain, raw steel had been rationed by the government. The biggest supplies went to manufacturers who could turn it into exportable goods. Brothers Maurice and Spencer Wilks, who controlled Rover, found a way around this.

Maurice had bought a war-surplus Willys Jeep to use on his farm, which gave him an idea: take the Jeep's outstanding off-road qualities and use them in a dual-role, 4x4 vehicle farmers would really value.

The first "Land Rover" prototype was a pick-up/tractor hybrid with its single, central seat, and stark functionality. It had Willys proportions because it actually used a Jeep body frame and axles. The Rover board gave cautious approval in September 1947

and, within a year, pilot production began. The Land Rover's bodywork was made from aluminum—cheap, plentiful, and, critically, unaffected by government restrictions. It was also light, giving great nimbleness on off-road terrain. Rover car components were used. The 80in (2m) wheelbase was retained, although later extended by 4in (10cm).

Early Land Rovers had a four-wheel drive system with no central differential and a freewheel in the front drive to reduce tire scrub. This was not so good for coming down hills, where the wheels turned at different speeds. In 1950, a dogleg clutch was added to give the driver two- or four-wheel drive.

Rover envisaged selling 50 a week as a sideline. Yet, within a year, Land Rovers were outselling Rover cars.

## SPECIFICATION

**YEAR REVEALED**  1948

**PLACE OF ORIGIN**  Solihull, Warwickshire, UK

**HISTORICAL STATUS**
production car

**ENGINE**  four-cylinder, 97ci (1,595cc)

**MAXIMUM POWER**  50bhp

**LAYOUT**  front-mounted engine driving all four wheels

**BODYWORK**  two- or four-door seven- or nine-seater utility and station wagon

**TOP SPEED**  56mph (90kph)

**NUMBER BUILT**  201,872

*"It must be along the lines of the Willys Jeep, but much more versatile, more useful as a power source, be able to do everything."*

MAURICE WILKS, ORIGINATOR OF THE LAND ROVER

How the Land Rover was first envisaged, with central driving position.

# PANHARD DYNAVIA

The Dynavia is a fascinating example of futuristic car design from over 60 years ago. But it was also meant to offer big benefits in everyday use, by increasing both performance and fuel consumption.

The impetus for the teardrop-shaped four-seater came from Panhard designer Louis Bionier, who set out, in 1944, to prove that such a car could be both stable and utterly practical. By 1945, he'd made a one-fifth-scale model which, under wind tunnel testing undertaken with help from the Institute Aérotechnique de Saint-Cyr, was found to have a phenomenally low drag.

The full-size model was slightly worse, but it was still slippery enough to boost the performance of the car, compared to the standard Panhard Dyna it was based on, by over a third. That meant a top speed of 87mph (140kph), and excellent fuel economy of 45mpg (16km/l). The carefully designed profile was also said to be good at resisting side winds and buffeting while overtaking.

Although audacious-looking, the Dynavia was twice overshadowed in 1948, first at the Paris motor show when the Citroën 2CV was the show-stopper, and again in London when the Jaguar XK120 and Morris Minor took the limelight. Still, one further example was built for a Panhard dealer in Grenoble, and this eventually sold to a private customer who used it on the road until it crashed, and was subsequently scrapped. But Bionier's research was not entirely wasted—the Dynavia had a strong influence on the design of the Panhard Dyna Z unveiled in 1953.

## SPECIFICATION

**YEAR REVEALED** 1948

**PLACE OF ORIGIN** Paris, France

**HISTORICAL STATUS** prototype

**ENGINE** flat two-cylinder, 37ci (610cc)

**MAXIMUM POWER** 28bhp

**LAYOUT** front-mounted engine driving the front wheels

**BODYWORK** two-door four-seater saloon

**TOP SPEED** 87mph (140kph)

**NUMBER BUILT** two

*"The front end treatment was one over-wrought assemblage taking in the headlamps, the bumpers, and the grille for the air intake."*

SERGE BELLU, FRENCH CAR HISTORIAN AND ILLUSTRATOR, ON THE DYNAVIA

The Panhard Dynavia was outstandingly aerodynamic and amazingly fast bearing in mind the tiny size of its two-cylinder engine.

Abdicated king of England, the Duke of Windsor, enjoys Palm Beach, Florida, with Wallis Simpson—and a new love in his life, a 1950 Buick Super station wagon.

The Tasco's cast-magnesium wheels were not easy to admire, because they were almost totally enclosed, but its "T-bar" roof was a novelty.

# TASCO

TASCO is an acronym for The American Sportscar Company, and the car pictured here shows the only example it ever managed to produce. The basis of the machine was a shortened 1948 Mercury chassis with a souped-up V8 engine.

The Tasco featured an enclosed cockpit like that of a light aircraft. Above the heads of driver and passenger were lift-out glass panels in the first-ever rendering of the "T-bar" roof (first seen in production in the Chevrolet Corvette of 1968). The cast-magnesium wheels were fully enclosed in their own fairings. The front two were made from fiberglass and turned with the wheels.

The car was created by a consortium of businessmen who hoped to sell replicas to wealthy sportsmen who would then campaign them in European-style sports car races held in New York State. They employed Gordon Buehrig to design it, an extremely talented stylist who had worked all over the American car industry but was most closely associated with the 1935 Auburn Speedster and 1936 Cord 810. Through his contacts, the bodywork was built by Derham, one of America's most respected luxury car body builders.

However, Buehrig was never happy with the Tasco, saying it was designed by a committee (the investors). He compared it to the failed Edsel as another lame duck. No doubt, car and design students today would disagree. Happily it can now be seen at the Auburn Cord Duesenberg Museum in Auburn, Indiana.

## SPECIFICATION

**YEAR REVEALED** 1948

**PLACE OF ORIGIN** Hartford, Connecticut

**HISTORICAL STATUS** prototype

**ENGINE** V8-cylinder, 239ci (3,917cc)

**MAXIMUM POWER** 100bhp-plus

**LAYOUT** front-mounted engine driving the rear wheels

**BODYWORK** two-door two-seater coupé

**TOP SPEED** unknown

**NUMBER BUILT** one

*"When the company folded, they owed me some money, and I said: 'Well, I want rights to that top'. So I went ahead at my own expense and got patents on the T Top."*

GORDON BUEHRIG, ORAL INTERVIEW HELD BY "AUTOMOBILE IN AMERICAN LIFE AND SOCIETY" PROJECT, 1984

# SAAB 92

Faced with a devastating drop in orders for its aircraft in 1945, Svenska Aeroplan AB (Swedish Aeroplane Limited) needed to diversify; it chose car manufacture. Inspiration came from the popularity of Germany's DKW cars in Sweden in the 1930s, where their surefooted roadholding suited the country's treacherous winter roads. But improving performance was a key goal; Saab aimed to make their car 50 percent faster by applying aircraft construction methods and aerodynamics.

The first prototype took six months to build in 1946. Three years of solid refinement and testing followed until the production lines began rolling on December 12, 1949. Impressively, just 17 percent (by value) of the car consisted of bought-in components.

Named the 92, it was a compact two-door, four-seater economy sedan with aerodynamic lines. It had a light, strong body built around a passenger "safety cell" and employed torsion bar suspension.

The power unit was Saab's own water-cooled two-stroke, a DKW clone mated to a three-speed gearbox with no synchromesh on first. To overcome the engine's Achilles heel (oil starvation during engine braking), the transmission featured a freewheel.

The 92 was certainly idiosyncratic. It came in just one color, green (gray, blue-grey, and black were added in 1953). The project's viability was assured when a major distributor pledged to buy 8,000 in exchange for exclusive Swedish sales rights; it soon had a 15,000-strong waiting list.

## SPECIFICATION

**YEAR REVEALED** 1949

**PLACE OF ORIGIN** Trollhättan, Sweden

**HISTORICAL STATUS** production car

**ENGINE** flat two-cylinder, 47ci (764cc)

**MAXIMUM POWER** 25bhp

**LAYOUT** front-mounted engine driving the front wheels

**BODYWORK** two-door four-seater sedan

**TOP SPEED** 65mph (105kph)

**NUMBER BUILT** 20,128

*"As a medium for putting in fantastic average speeds over rough, twisty roads, it has few rivals in its class. The Saab 92 is definitely a sports car in spirit."*

THE AUTOCAR MAGAZINE, 1949

The Saab aircraft company took a long, hard look at the post-World War II environment and created the economical 92 car to capitalize on it.

# 3

# THE JET-PROPELLED, CHROME-PLATED ERA

Throughout the whole of the 1950s, and despite post-war privations and fuel crises, the automobile became the center of attention like never before; car ownership was still not universal, and roads around the world were relatively traffic-free. However, by the close of the decade, exuberant motoring freedom would be on the way out, forever.

Carmakers in America highlighted the speed, luxury, and power of their products by harnessing aerospace imagery and chromium-plated decoration in about equal measure. The results were often breathtaking, sometimes absurd. Across the Atlantic in Europe, with resources still scarce after World War II, the emphasis was on attractive economy cars, or else stirring sports and racing machines from Italy, Germany, and Britain. There was also the prospect of an emerging Japanese car industry.

Cars were getting more user-friendly, too. They had to be, as multi-lane highways criss-crossed entire continents and demanded new levels of mechanical resilience for sustained high-speed driving over ever-greater distances.

# ROVER "JET 1"

The crowds at the Festival of Britain exhibition on London's South Bank in 1951 must have sensed that Britain's motor industry was on top of its game. For here was a car demonstrating Britain had the technology and ingenuity to keep pace with America and Europe. It was Rover's "Jet 1," the world's first gas turbine car—an open two-seater, using body panels that were recognizably adapted from the Rover 75 sedan, and offering seamless delivery of power to the wheels.

In 1952, it established a new speed record at 151.96mph (244.56kph) for the flying kilometer. Although several companies would also build turbine cars,

Rover badge

none would pursue the technology like Rover, with its long series of prototypes stretching into the mid-1960s. For the small Jet 1 project team, led by Spencer King and Frank Bell, there were numerous obstacles: the engine turned at 26,000rpm, five times higher than most car engines in the early 1950s; it was air-cooled; and had no internal engine braking. These hurdles were overcome, but two problems proved insurmountable: exceptionally high fuel consumption and the huge costs of making such an engine. However, the technology was soon exploited commercially by Rover Gas Turbine Engines Ltd and for Britain, the Rover Jet 1 was a true flag-waver.

## SPECIFICATION

**YEAR REVEALED** 1950

**PLACE OF ORIGIN** Solihull, Warwickshire, UK

**HISTORICAL STATUS** prototype

**ENGINE** gas turbine

**MAXIMUM POWER** 230bhp

**LAYOUT** rear-mounted engine driving the rear wheels

**BODYWORK** two-door, two-seater roadster

**TOP SPEED** 151mph (244kph)

**NUMBER BUILT** one

*"With a peculiar and rather eerie high-pitched whistle just behind my left ear, I cautiously pressed the accelerator. I was just about to ask what was wrong when I realized that, almost imperceptibly, we had begun to move."*

HAROLD HASTINGS, *THE MOTOR* MAGAZINE, 1955

Although similar on the outside to Rover's other catalog products, the large air intakes near the rear wheels hint at the jet power inside.

# TRIUMPH TRX

It was known as the "new Roadster," or by its nickname "Silver Bullet," but for Triumph, the official and futuristic TRX proved nothing but trouble.

The smooth-lined two-seater, unveiled in 1950, was meant as a replacement for the Triumph 2000 Roadster, a delightfully old-fashioned model with its tiny cockpit, dickey seat, and huge, free-standing headlamps. Seeking a more progressive image, Triumph stylist Walter Belgrove came up with the TRX's sleek, torpedo-like profile, which was built in double-skinned aluminum. To maintain the flowing look, headlamps were concealed behind revolving metal covers, and the rear wheels were artfully faired-in. The new car was loaded with power-assisted gadgets. Windows, radio aerial, headlight covers, and the side-opening hood were electrically operated, and the overdrive on the three-speed gearbox was electro-hydraulically driven. A large electric motor drove the system, whose network was carefully sandwiched inside the double-skinned bodywork. With so much complexity, the Silver Bullet was plagued with problems. Soon plans were ditched, and Triumph turned to the simple TR2 sports car.

## SPECIFICATION

**YEAR REVEALED** 1950

**PLACE OF ORIGIN** Coventry, Warwickshire, UK

**HISTORICAL STATUS** prototype

**ENGINE** four-cylinder, 127ci 2, (088cc)

**MAXIMUM POWER** 72bhp

**LAYOUT** front-mounted engine driving the rear wheels

**BODYWORK** two-door, two-seater roadster

**TOP SPEED** 90mph (145kph) (projected)

**NUMBER BUILT** three

*"When he pressed a button to raise the window, the seat slid back, and when he pressed the seat adjustment button, the hood was promptly raised."*

PHILIP TURNER, *MOTOR* MAGAZINE, 1973

The sheer quantity of gadgets, such as the electrically-operated hood, was the ultimate downfall of the TRX.

# CHRYSLER K-310

A frenzied round of trans-Atlantic dealing between America's Chrysler Corporation and Italy's Carrozzeria Ghia preceded the unveiling of this handsome coupé in 1952.

Originally, Fiat sought Chrysler's help in training its manufacturing technicians. Then Chrysler realized that Italy's car-styling brilliance could help to upgrade its image. Ghia and Pinin Farina both tendered for the business by building one-off bodies. Ghia's car, the Plymouth XX-500 sedan, was no beauty, but Chrysler was impressed at the workmanship and modest cost. Soon Chrysler's American-designed prototypes were brought to life in Ghia's Turin workshops. The K-310 was the first commission with a design overseen by

Virgil Exner, Chrysler's "ideas man." "K" commemorated Kaufman Keller, Chrysler's president, and "310" denoted its supposed power (although the engine in the Chrysler Saratoga chassis only gave 180bhp). Ghia duly translated the drawings and scale models into a completely hand-built, full-size car—for just $20,000. Exner had made features out of normally concealed components, such as the spare-wheel shape molded into the boot lid. The large wheels emphasized the car's rakish lines, while the small, egg-crate-style radiator grille highlighted the low hood line. With the K-310, Chrysler showed it could design cars every bit as exciting as those from Ford and General Motors. And they had the added cachet of being "Made In Italy."

## SPECIFICATION

**YEAR REVEALED** 1952

**PLACE OF ORIGIN** Detroit, Michigan, and Turin, Italy

**HISTORICAL STATUS** prototype

**ENGINE** V8-cylinder, 331ci (5,424cc)

**MAXIMUM POWER** 180bhp

**LAYOUT** front-mounted engine driving the rear wheels

**BODYWORK** two-door, five-seater coupé

**TOP SPEED** unknown

**NUMBER BUILT** one

*"The wheel is one of mankind's greatest inventions. Why attempt to hide it?"* VIRGIL EXNER, CHRYSLER CHIEF DESIGNER

The huge wheels of Chrysler's **K-310** show car helped to emphasise its rakish appearance.

This Pegaso Z-102's beautiful coachwork was by Carrozzeria Touring, and was similar to the Italian designer's later work for the Aston Martin DB4.

# PEGASO Z-102

At the 1951 Paris salon, the debut of the Pegaso, an exclusive and sophisticated sports car from Spain, set the automotive world buzzing. Designed by Wilfredo Ricart—recently back in his native Barcelona after nine years as Alfa Romeo's chief engineer—the Pegaso, like so many of Ricart's projects, was a magnificent folly.

On his return to Spain in 1946, Ricart joined ENASA, an arm of the Instituto Nacional de Industria formed by the Spanish government to counter a crippling shortage of trucks. Four years later, he directed his energies with the engineering department to create an advanced GT car. At the heart of this brave project was a dry-sump double overhead-camshaft alloy V8 with optional supercharging. It featured a five-speed gearbox. The Pegaso's strong platform chassis was fitted with a variety of exotic bodies, the majority by Saoutchik, but the more attractive coupé and spyders by Touring of Milan. Pegaso's own coupé was crude and slab-sided in comparison. Two coupés were entered for Le Mans in 1953 but failed to even start, and a 195ci (3,200cc) spyder performed well on the 1954 Carrera PanAmericana until catching fire after a spectacular accident. A twin-hull record machine called "El Bisiluro," however, reached 242.9kph (150.9mph) on the Jabbeke motorway in Belgium. The era of these complex, costly and often temperamental machines was limited. When Ricart retired in 1958, Pegaso returned to its main business of trucks and buses.

## SPECIFICATION

**YEAR REVEALED** 1951

**PLACE OF ORIGIN** Barcelona, Spain

**HISTORICAL STATUS** production car

**ENGINE** V8-cylinder, 151–194ci (2,473–3,178cc)

**MAXIMUM POWER** 190bhp (194ci/3,178cc)

**LAYOUT** front-mounted engine driving the rear wheels

**BODYWORK** two-door, two-seater roadster and coupé

**TOP SPEED** 120mph (172ci /2,816cc)

**NUMBER BUILT** 100 (estimated)

*"The Pegaso, for a year or two the world's fastest car, was the first road car powered by a V8 engine with four camshafts; it was once described as 'a staggering noise machine.'"*

BRIAN SEWELL, ART CRITIC, IN *THE INDEPENDENT* NEWSPAPER, 2007

Driven off the line on November 23, 1954, this gold-plated Chevrolet Bel-Air Sport Coupé stuns onlookers in Flint, Michigan, US. It took the corporation 46 years to reach this epic tally.

# BENTLEY R-TYPE CONTINENTAL

In the ration-book Britain of the early 1950s, the sight of a Bentley Continental must have slackened many a jaw.

Here was one of motoring's ultimates: the fastest genuine four-seater car in the world—it could top 120mph (193kph) effortlessly—and one of the most beautiful. Shaped in Rolls-Royce's Hucknall wind tunnel, Crewe's flagship was an owner-driver super-coupé, its bold, distinctive fastback profile influenced, although no one would admit it, by the 1948 Cadillac 62 Coupé. The Bentley grille still stood proud and tall but the tail fins kept the Continental tracking straight at high speed. The Continental's alloy bodywork was built in London by H. J. Mulliner on a special high performance chassis. The 279ci (4,566cc) engine breathed more freely than in the standard R-type sedan thanks to a higher compression ratio and a big bore exhaust. Gearing was higher, and the scuttle and steering column lower to achieve a sleeker line. The weight-loss regime for the first sporting Bentley since the 1930s included aluminum bumpers (rather than steel) and lightweight-alloy bucket seat frames. But passengers still traveled in style: there was room for four occupants to travel in lavish leather surroundings; and the driver enjoyed a full set of instruments including rev-counter and oil temperature gauge. On the road, the Continental had a fantastically long stride, with 80mph (129kph) in second gear, and 120mph (193kph) in top gear. For the seriously rich, there was no faster way of escaping the gray skies of post-war Britain.

## SPECIFICATION

**YEAR REVEALED** 1952

**PLACE OF ORIGIN** Crewe, Cheshire and London, UK

**HISTORICAL STATUS** production car

**ENGINE** six-cylinder, 279–298ci (4,566–4,887cc)

**MAXIMUM POWER** 158–172bhp

**LAYOUT** front-mounted engine driving the rear wheels

**BODYWORK** two-door, four-seater coupé

**TOP SPEED** 124mph (200kph) (298ci /4,887cc)

**NUMBER BUILT** 208

*"I drive my Continental for therapy, and still have no trouble with salesmen in Vauxhalls on the motorway. It's the nicest pure Bentley ever made."*

BRITISH FORMER MP ALAN CLARK IN *BACKFIRE*, HIS MOTORING DIARIES, 2001

A top speed of almost 124mph (200kph), a sumptuous interior, and a streamlined shape made the original Bentley Continental very desirable.

# DODGE FIREARROW

The talented Virgil Exner, heading up Chrysler design in the 1950s, was certainly a hard worker. The outflow of plans from his drawing board for exciting new cars appeared unstoppable, as did the capacity of Italian coachbuilder Ghia—his preferred contractor—to turn them into fully functioning prototypes.

The Firearrow was a sleek roadster created in 1953. Its impressively clean lines—with wheels tucked neatly inside a wide roadster body and a bullet-shaped ornament in the center of its radiator grille—were up-to-the-minute. It was stunning in bright red, with a polished metal belt-line and a handmade wooden steering wheel. Presented under the Dodge brand, the first car was a full-size mock-up, but a similar working car in yellow, with its racy wire wheels, was a star turn at a 1954 "Harmony On Wheels" exhibition. This was rapidly followed by the Firearrow III coupé and the four-seater Firearrow and Firebomb convertibles, with black-and-white checkerboard upholstery. The closed car was timed at 143mph (230kph), driven by leading female stunt pilot Betty Skelton. The five show cars were initially intended to grab headlines and to lift Dodge's staid image. But they led to a limited production run of 117 Firebomb replicas, privately financed by Dual Motors of Detroit, US, and sold as the Dual-Ghia. They were popular trophy assets among movie stars and politicians—in terms of glamour alone, Exner and Chrysler must have been delighted with the "Firearrow effect".

## SPECIFICATION

**YEAR REVEALED** 1953

**PLACE OF ORIGIN** Detroit, Michigan, and Turin, Italy

**HISTORICAL STATUS** prototype

**ENGINE** V8-cylinder, 241ci (3,954cc)

**MAXIMUM POWER** 152bhp

**LAYOUT** front-mounted engine driving the rear wheels

**BODYWORK** two-door, two-seater roadster, four-seater coupé and four-seater convertible

**TOP SPEED** 143mph (230kph) (Firearrow III)

**NUMBER BUILT** four

*"The Ghia line of these cars brought a note of gracefulness to these elephantine American chassis, reducing the mass of chrome components to rational proportions."*

TORINO MOTORI MAGAZINE

The polished metal belt-line and bright red coachwork added to the Dodge Firearrow's raciness.

The Isetta's entire front panel swung open to give access to the "bubble" car's interior, while the rear wheels were set a mere 20in (51cm) apart.

# ISETTA

Bubble cars were a European fad in the 1950s. These tiny, cramped contraptions offered minimal motoring and a meager thirst for fuel in the guise of a brand new car. The nickname came from the cars' commonly characteristic ovular shape. The Isetta set the trend for bubble cars, but it was later followed by other makers, including Fuldamobil, Heinkel, Messerschmitt, and Scootacar. The concept came from an Italian refrigerator manufacturer called Isotherm. The main idea was for a "cabin scooter," a blend of the thrift of Italy's Vespa, but with weather protection and accommodation for a young family. It was devised as a four-wheeler, but the rear wheels were just 20in (51cm) apart. The only door was at the front, where the entire snub-fronted nose swung outward, taking the cleverly articulated steering column with it.

The tiny, twin-cylinder engine was at the back, while the driver sat on the left, to counterbalance it. Italian drivers were none too keen on the Iso Isetta, and the company stopped making it after two years. But BMW took out a licence to make the car in Munich with larger capacity engines.

With later improvements, it proved amazingly successful among German buyers. The little car is widely said to have "saved" BMW from financial ruin.

BMW badge

## SPECIFICATION

**YEAR REVEALED** 1953

**PLACE OF ORIGIN** Milan, Italy, and Munich, Germany

**HISTORICAL STATUS** production car

**ENGINE** flat-two-cylinder, 14ci (236cc) and single-cylinder, 15–18ci (247–298cc)

**MAXIMUM POWER** 13bhp (298cc/18ci)

**LAYOUT** rear-mounted engine driving the rear wheels

**BODYWORK** single-door, four-seater sedan

**TOP SPEED** 50mph (80kph)

**NUMBER BUILT** 197,575

*"The noise level is closely related to the speed and throttle opening... a strong headwind has a pronounced effect on performance, and the noise rises accordingly."*

THE MOTOR MAGAZINE ROAD TEST, 1957

# JOWETT JUPITER R4

Motoring history is littered with marques that failed despite customer loyalty and interesting products. Jowett is a prime example, and this little sports car was its last gasp. Had the Jupiter R4 entered production in 1954, as planned, it would have been the first British car with a body made of fiberglass—the plastic laminate pioneered by Chevrolet's 1953 Corvette.

The Jowett Javelin, an advanced family car, had caused a real stir in 1947. The Jupiter roadster that followed three years later used the Javelin's flat-four overhead-valve engine in a special spaceframe chassis. In various forms, the Jupiter then enjoyed a stellar motor-sport career, including class wins on the 1951 Monte Carlo Rally and the 1952 Le Mans 24-hour endurance race. This was all far removed from Jowett's stock-in-trade, a line of basic twin-cylinder delivery vans. But sports cars made promising export material. The short-chassis R4 was intended to capitalize on the Jupiter's reputation, with a body style copying the rare and exotic Ferrari 166 Barchetta. One all-steel prototype and two experimental plastic R4s were built, all boasting overdrive and an electric engine cooling fan. They were the work of Roy Lunn, later closely involved in developing the Ford GT40. Sadly, though, a decision to start manufacturing its own gearboxes proved disastrous for Jowett—the high level of rejects bringing Javelin and Jupiter assembly to a halt. The resulting cashflow problems brought the firm down, and the R4 with it.

## SPECIFICATION

**YEAR REVEALED** 1953

**PLACE OF ORIGIN** Bradford, Yorkshire, UK

**HISTORICAL STATUS** prototype

**ENGINE** flat-four-cylinder, 91ci (1,486cc)

**MAXIMUM POWER** 64bhp

**LAYOUT** front-mounted engine driving the rear wheels

**BODYWORK** two-door, two-seater roadster

**TOP SPEED** 100mph (161kph)

**NUMBER BUILT** three

*"The exhibits on the Jowett stand at Earl's Court will comprise the Javelin, the Jupiter, and an entirely new sports model called the R4 Jupiter… Hope has not been abandoned that delivery will be recommenced in the not too distant future."*

THE MOTOR MAGAZINE, LONDON MOTOR SHOW PREVIEW 1953

Fiberglass body panels meant that the sporty Jupiter R4 could be produced cheaply, but it came too late to save the Yorkshire-based company.

An astonishing example of automotive design and the craft of the coachbuilder, the **BAT 7** celebrated Bertone's partnership with Alfa Romeo.

# BERTONE/ALFA ROMEO BAT 7

BAT stands for *Berlinetta Aerodinamica Tecnica*—the codename given to three experimental Alfa Romeo 1900s, each handbuilt in the 1950s. They were the work of young Italian Franco Scaglione, employed by the renowned coachbuilding company Bertone. The project extended a joint venture between Alfa Romeo and Bertone, in which the rapidly expanding (yet family-owned) coachbuilder designed and built bodies for Alfa's Giulietta Sprint GT.

Designer Scaglione's aims were to reduce drag when a car was turning, increase frontal downforce, and create shapes that produced minimum turbulence. Another of the parameters was to take a chassis with a 100bhp engine, similar to the 90bhp Alfa 1900, and make it capable of 125mph (201kph). BAT 5, constructed in 1953, recorded an excellent drag coefficient of 0.23, but BAT 7, built a year later and shown here, was even more wind-cheating, at 0.19. No car on sale today can better BAT 7's aerodynamics. Nor its drama—its gigantic tailfins were like scrolled metal, their rising profile and inward curve sheer automotive theater, and the contours of windshield, wheel apertures, and copious air intakes created a car of endless visual fascination. BAT 9 was never scientifically tested in the same way, but unlike earlier incarnations, it was a practical road machine that covered thousands of miles. Overall, the main legacy of the BAT trio was a demonstration of Bertone's mastery of metal-shaping.

## SPECIFICATION

**YEAR REVEALED** 1954

**PLACE OF ORIGIN** Milan and Turin, Italy

**HISTORICAL STATUS** prototype

**ENGINE** four-cylinder, 121ci (1,975cc)

**MAXIMUM POWER** 100bhp

**LAYOUT** front-mounted engine driving the rear wheels

**BODYWORK** two-door, two-seater coupé

**TOP SPEED** 125mph (201kph)

**NUMBER BUILT** one

*"The car seemed very stable at high speeds, and tended to straighten up automatically after cornering at sustained speeds."*

*MOTOR ITALIA* MAGAZINE, 1954, ON BAT 5

# CADILLAC EL CAMINO

There's an embarrassment of riches when it comes to extraordinary Cadillacs, but this racy number is a highly significant car. It heralded several key design features that became synonymous with Cadillac's production cars of the late 1950s.

The El Camino—short for El Camino Real, or Royal Highway, another name for America's Highway 101—was one of a trio of Cadillac show cars, together with the Cadillac LaEspada and Park Avenue. They were part of the 1954 Motorama, General Motors' traveling showcase of futuristic concept cars that toured the US that year. The El Camino's distinctive roof styling, with fiberglass "saddles," a brushed aluminum top, and curved glass, previewed the Cadillac Eldorado Brougham of 1955,

while the tailfin designs were also introduced gradually from 1955 until every Caddy had them by 1958. It was similar for the wing-like bumpers culminating in bullet-tipped overriders and the quadruple headlights—all universal on Cadillacs by 1958. The pearlescent silver painted El Camino paved the way, and softened the impact of some radical styling ideas of the near-future. General Motors' press release for the car frothed with hyperbole, explaining how the car was "regally styled to blaze across the highways of our great land." Ironically, though, it was a non-running mock-up, made from fiberglass. The compact El Camino hinted at a Cadillac luxury two-seater to come, but no such model hit showrooms until the Allante of 1987.

## SPECIFICATION

**YEAR REVEALED** 1954

**PLACE OF ORIGIN** Detroit, Michigan

**HISTORICAL STATUS** prototype

**ENGINE** V8-cylinder, 331ci (5,422cc)

**MAXIMUM POWER** 230bhp

**LAYOUT** front-mounted engine driving the rear wheels

**BODYWORK** two-door, two-seater coupé

**TOP SPEED** unknown

**NUMBER BUILT** one

*"This is a two-passenger hardtop coupé bearing a Spanish name which means 'the highway' and features what its designers term 'aircraft styling' and 'supersonic' tail-fins on the rear fenders."*

MOTOR LIFE MAGAZINE, 1954

Cadillac's compact El Camino coupé would never reach showrooms, but its styling and gimmicks did find their way on to production models.

# FERGUSON R4

In 1954, this dumpy-looking sedan was probably the most advanced, and safest, family car in the world. It heralded a visionary project started by colorful Irish tractor tycoon Harry Ferguson. In one of many business battles, Ferguson had fallen out with Ford over American tractor design patents, and in 1952, he won $9.25 million in a legal settlement with the Detroit giant. A year later, he'd merged his Ferguson Tractors firm with a Canadian rival, which gave him $16 million-worth of shares in the new Massey-Harris-Ferguson business.

But instead of relishing his pension, the 66-year-old Ferguson had founded Harry Ferguson Research in 1950. His conviction was that everyday cars could be made much safer in wet or slippery road conditions if they had four-wheel drive, and he was soon joined by racing driver Tony Rolt and ex-Aston Martin designer Claude Hill. By the time the R4 was completed in 1954, the evolving prototype had another important innovation: the world's first anti-lock brakes, developed with Dunlop and called Maxaret. This technical package gave the car spectacular safety advantages, and led to the even more impressive 1959 R5 research vehicle, a proper rolling billboard in estate car form. In 1966, the exclusive Jensen FF became the first production car to use Ferguson's four-wheel drive and skid-proof braking. In 1980, the package finally reached mainstream family cars with the American Motors Eagle range. Sadly, Ferguson didn't see any of this—he died in 1960.

## SPECIFICATION

**YEAR REVEALED** 1954

**PLACE OF ORIGIN** Redhill, Surrey, UK

**HISTORICAL STATUS** prototype

**ENGINE** flat-four-cylinder, 134ci (2,200cc)

**MAXIMUM POWER** unknown

**LAYOUT** front-mounted engine driving all four wheels

**BODYWORK** four-seater sedan

**TOP SPEED** unknown

**NUMBER BUILT** one

*"The safety limits of this car on slippery roads are quite remarkably high. Whatever we did, and we tried quite hard, we failed completely to get ourselves into any sort of trouble at all."*

ROAD TEST OF FERGUSON PROTOTYPE (R5), *MOTOR* MAGAZINE, 1966

Slippery conditions were just the kind of thing the Ferguson R4 sought to conquer, with the extra road adhesion supplied by four-wheel drive.

Test driver Mauri Rose is here seen at the wheel of the Firebird XP-21, putting the space-age prototype through its paces in Arizona in 1954.

# GENERAL MOTORS FIREBIRD XP-21

You couldn't buy it, much less drive it on the road, but General Motors was determined to prove its faith in the future with this winged wonder powered by America's first automotive gas turbine.

General Motors hired the Indianapolis Speedway for a day, where the car's project leader Emmett Conklin had driven it at up to 100mph (161kph) before the tires lost traction and his nerve broke. The Firebird was not for the faint-hearted: the 370bhp "Whirlfire Turbo-Power" turbine behind the driver ran at a blurry 13,300rpm, taking its power from compressed gas burned in a gasifier which spun at 26,000rpm; the exhaust reached temperatures of 1,251°F (677°C); and braking came from drums on the wheels and flaps in the "wings".

The Firebird toured the US as part of the 1954 Motorama roadshow, feeding the public's "jet age" obsession. The styling of this aircraft-on-wheels easily met "wow factor" expectations. The work of legendary GM design chief Harley Earl, it was fashioned after the Douglas Skyray supersonic plane and made from fiberglass, like the brand new Chevrolet Corvette. The plastic cockpit bubble was pure B-movie science fiction. A year later, Firebird II was unveiled, a four-seater, rendering the XP-21, retrospectively, Firebird I. Claiming "the future is our assignment," General Motors presented the two-seater Firebird III in 1958 which, with its refined drivetrain, cruise control, and anti-lock brakes was even more of a rolling laboratory than its predecessors.

## SPECIFICATION

**YEAR REVEALED** 1954

**PLACE OF ORIGIN** Detroit, Michigan

**HISTORICAL STATUS** prototype

**ENGINE** gas turbine

**MAXIMUM POWER** 370bhp

**LAYOUT** rear-mounted engine driving the rear wheels

**BODYWORK** canopy-entry, single-seater coupé

**TOP SPEED** unknown

**NUMBER BUILT** one

*"Never did I have the impression the car would fishtail, swerve, or swing from one side to another. And it never did."*

MAURI ROSE, TEST DRIVER, ON THE FIREBIRD

The Metropolitan was designed in the US but built in Britain; this is the later 1500 version in the Austin trim in which it was also sold in the UK.

# NASH/AUSTIN METROPOLITAN

Nash Motors had been mulling a really small "sub-compact" car since 1945, when it asked freelance Detroit designer William Flajole to work up some proposals. Market research was in its infancy, but Nash decided to consult the public in 1949, to canvass opinion of Flajole's drawings for a small car, the NXI (Nash Experimental International).

The answer from the suburbs reflected America's changing demographics: it must be cheap as well as dainty because an NX1 would be used mostly as a second car for shopping. Convinced of a good market, Nash gave it the green light. The company had no experience of building small cars, no suitable components, and no spare factory space. Rather than change the formula, they chose a European sub-contractor, Austin, who had the ideal 73ci (1,200cc) engine and three-speed gearbox, from its A40 Somerset, and was eager to build cars for an export market on the other side of the Atlantic. The Nash Metropolitan went on sale in the US and Canada in March 1954. It came as a two-door convertible or hardtop; the latter in two-tone paint. In 1956, a larger engine headlined detail and styling improvements. Then in April 1957, Austin launched the car in Britain, where its vibrant colors and looks set it apart.

*Austin badge*

## SPECIFICATION

**YEAR REVEALED** 1954

**PLACE OF ORIGIN** Kenosha, Wisconsin, and Birmingham, UK

**HISTORICAL STATUS** production car

**ENGINE** four-cylinder, 73–91ci (1,200–1,489cc)

**MAXIMUM POWER** 47bhp

**LAYOUT** front-mounted engine driving the rear wheels

**BODYWORK** two-door, two-seater convertible and hardtop

**TOP SPEED** 75mph (121kph) (1,489cc)

**NUMBER BUILT** 104,377

*"It is not a sports car by the weirdest torturing of the imagination, but it is a fleet, sporty little bucket which should prove just what the doctor ordered for a second car."*

TOM MCCAHILL, *MECHANIX ILLUSTRATED* MAGAZINE, 1954

# JAGUAR D-TYPE

By the early 1950s, Jaguar exuded excitement on all fronts: its XK engine was acclaimed; it built the most glamorous sedans available; and the XK120 sports car was world-famous on road and track.

Still, it was apparent to company founder William Lyons that a production car could no longer compete in the highest motorsport echelons. So Jaguar's racing department devised a special-bodied XK120, the XK120C or C-type (for Competition). It twice won Le Mans and, furthermore, proved the effectiveness of disc brakes. The first three World Champion drivers, Farina, Fangio, and Ascari, all bought one to use as road cars. Jaguar was interested in really conquering Le Mans—anything else was a bonus—and pursued that determinedly in 1954 with its first pure racing car, the D-type. It featured purpose-designed monocoque construction, all-round disc brakes (Jaguar and Dunlop refined them together), and bodywork designed by aerodynamicist Malcolm Sayer. The stabilizing fin behind the driver's head was a D-type hallmark. On its 1954 Le Mans debut, a D-type finished a close second to a Ferrari with a much larger engine. Thus proven in public, Jaguar offered it to privateer drivers—it cost £1,895, before tax—and soon D-types were winning races worldwide. The pinnacle of its career was three successive wins at Le Mans, 1955–57. In 1957, five cars entered and they finished 1-2-3-4-6—one of the most remarkable Le Mans performances ever.

## SPECIFICATION

**YEAR REVEALED** 1954

**PLACE OF ORIGIN** Coventry, Warwickshire, UK

**HISTORICAL STATUS** sports-racing car

**ENGINE** six-cylinder, 210ci (3,442cc)

**MAXIMUM POWER** 250bhp

**LAYOUT** front-mounted engine driving the rear wheels

**BODYWORK** two-door, two-seater roadster

**TOP SPEED** 175mph (282kph)

**NUMBER BUILT** 71

*"The brilliant success of the Jaguars in taking the first four and sixth places becomes all the more significant when it is considered that every one of these cars was a private entry."*

THE AUTOCAR MAGAZINE REPORT ON THE LE MANS RACE, 1957

This is the D-type co-driven by Ron Flockhart and Ivor Bueb on its way to victory in the 1957 Le Mans 24-hour race, Jaguar's fifth victory there.

# MASSERATI 250F

Founded in 1926, Maserati was purely a manufacturer of racing cars for its first 20 years. By 1934, it was the planet's largest builder of single-seater racers. The 250F was the result of unique expertise in Grand Prix/ Formula One techniques.

Adhering to the sport's rules for 153ci (2,500cc) cars, the 250F boasted a competent tubular chassis frame, independent wishbone/coil spring front suspension, and a light De Dion tubular rear axle. The centerpiece of the car was its superb engine, a straight-six, un-supercharged unit derived from Maserati's A6

Formula Two, but with increased capacity, and three twin-choke Weber carburetors. The revamped 1957-season 250Fs came with a five-speed gearbox, fuel injection, more power, better brakes, and even more svelte bodywork. Juan Manuel Fangio's victory at the Nürburgring in the German Grand Prix of August 1957 was epic, his 250F four-wheel drifting its way up the field in the second half of the race to catch and overtake Peter Collins's leading Ferrari. It was the car's finest hour and a 5th World Championship for Fangio. In terms of mixing balance with speed, the 250F was just about the best.

## SPECIFICATION

**YEAR REVEALED**  1954

**PLACE OF ORIGIN**  Modena, Italy

**HISTORICAL STATUS**  Formula One racing car

**ENGINE**  six-cylinder, 152ci (2,490cc)

**MAXIMUM POWER**  220–270bhp

**LAYOUT**  front-mounted engine driving the rear wheels

**BODYWORK**  single-seater racer

**TOP SPEED**  185mph (298kph)

**NUMBER BUILT**  34

*"I have never driven that quickly before in my life and I don't think I will ever be able to do it again."*

JUAN MANUEL FANGIO IN 1957, AFTER HIS EPIC GERMAN GRAND PRIX WIN IN THE 250F

Stirling Moss drives a Maserati 250F in August 1954; Moss and Fangio would soon propel the 250F to Formula One stardom.

# MERCEDES-BENZ 300SL

The Mercedes 300SL was the first true "supercar," a high-tech, 150mph (241kph) road machine built expressly for high-speed driving.

However, prototypes of the car were pure competition machines, bearing the internal codename of W194. In 1952, these 300SLs won the two most gruelling endurance races of the day—the Le Mans 24-hour race and the Carrera Panamericana. Their complex tubular spaceframe chassis, under an aluminum body, had unusually high sills, and Mercedes-Benz overcame cockpit access problems with spectacular "gull-wing" doors. Hinged at the top of the roof's apex, they opened outwards and upwards, and resembled a flying seabird when both were up together. Mercedes' US importer pressed for a production version of this exciting car, and in 1954 the German factory obliged with the 300SL. Far more elegant with its elongated tail and heavy chrome bumpers, blistered wheelarches were also added to aid aerodynamic stability at high speed. The 180bhp of the hottest racing 300SLs was upped to 215bhp thanks to Bosch fuel injection, a world first on a production car. It was costly, with a price tag twice that of comparable cars, such as the Jaguar XK140. The 300SL was the preserve of the super-rich, and a favorite with celebrities and off-duty racing drivers. However, its suspect "swing axle" rear suspension needed expert skills on twisty roads. Many petrified new owners found themselves heading for roadside undergrowth—backward.

## SPECIFICATION

**YEAR REVEALED** 1954

**PLACE OF ORIGIN** Stuttgart, Germany

**HISTORICAL STATUS** production car

**ENGINE** six-cylinder, 183ci 2, (996cc)

**MAXIMUM POWER** 215bhp

**LAYOUT** front-mounted engine driving the rear wheels

**BODYWORK** two-door, two-seater coupé

**TOP SPEED** 150mph (241kph)

**NUMBER BUILT** 1,400

Fuel-injection gave the 300SL stunning performance.

*"Admittedly, they may have wondered what it was that passed them, but by that time the Mercedes 300SL is over the hills and far away!"*

THE AUTOCAR MAGAZINE ROAD TEST, 1955

The novel "gull-wing" doors were there to preserve chassis rigidity rather than impress the neighbors!

Stirling Moss at Aintree, UK, in the second-generation, "open wheel" Mercedes-Benz W196, heading for a win there in the British Grand Prix.

# MERCEDES-BENZ W196

Mercedes-Benz made a spectacular return to top-level motor sport in 1954, 20 years after the three-pointed star was first seen in Grand Prix racing. In 1950, the international series had been reorganized as Formula One, with a world championship for drivers. The first four years were dominated first by Alfa Romeo and then Ferrari.

Mercedes adopted the new regulations for 152ci (2,497cc) un-supercharged cars with its W196, notable for its wind-cheating, all-enveloping body and a special mechanical valve-operating system in its slanted, straight-eight, fuel-injected engine. The car showed such promise that Fangio defected from Maserati to Mercedes during the 1954 season, driving it to victory in their very first Grand Prix (GP) outing together at Reims in France. Yet, after a poor finish in the British GP, the Argentinian master declared the full-width bodywork a hindrance, saying he couldn't place the front wheels accurately. So for the German GP, at the Nürburgring, a conventional, open-wheel W196 was provided, starting a string of victories. Mercedes, indeed, varied the W196 design depending on the circuit, including a short wheelbase for Stirling Moss's winning drive—his first ever—in the 1955 British GP. That year, a Mercedes-Benz 300SLR sports car, a W196 derivative driven by Pierre Levegh, crashed into a grandstand at Le Mans, killing 87. The terrible carnage moved Mercedes to withdraw from motor racing altogether; the W196 having won an unprecedent nine out of 12 races entered.

## SPECIFICATION

**YEAR REVEALED**  1954

**PLACE OF ORIGIN**  Stuttgart, Germany

**HISTORICAL STATUS**  Formula One racing car

**ENGINE**  eight-cylinder, 152ci (2,497cc)

**MAXIMUM POWER**  257–290bhp

**LAYOUT**  front-mounted engine driving the rear wheels

**BODYWORK**  single-seater racer

**TOP SPEED**  150mph (241kph)

**NUMBER BUILT**  ten

*"It was reasonable to expect the 1954 Formula One team to be the equal of any of its rivals."*

DENIS JENKINSON, *MOTOR SPORT* MAGAZINE, 1954

Mercedes-Benz gave the W196 a custom-made transporter.

Ghia's Gilda show car was a wedge-shaped façade totally lacking running gear, although the car has today been converted to gas turbine power.

# GHIA GILDA

This extreme study in automobile aerodynamics was the center of attention at the 1955 Turin motor show, where it rotated majestically and silently on a spacious turntable before startled visitors.

Ghia's Gilda came together after collaboration between the Turin Polytechnic and Giovanni Savonuzzi, a designer recently recruited from Cisitalia. Starting in November 1954 with scale models and eventually progressing to the full-size car, it was extensively wind-tested to overcome what Savonuzzi called "the imperfectly understood science" of streamlining. The Gilda was as impractical an everyday proposition as many other styling exercises, with its two huge fins rising arrow-like along each of its lengthy flanks, its enclosed wheels, and its unfeasibly slim roof pillars. None of which mattered, of course, because this was a show car, pure and simple. Still, it didn't stop Ghia claiming the car had the potential to hit 140mph (225kph) if fitted with a tuned OSCA engine, when in fact, no drivetrain was installed at all inside the tubular steel-framed, aluminum panelled façade. The publicity machine rolled on after its circuit of European motor shows. The car was offered free to the Henry Ford Museum in Dearborn, Michigan, and in October 1955, it was sent to the US. In 1956, Ghia built two further cars directly inspired by what it now termed the "Gilda Line"— the Ghia Dart and an incredible Ferrari 410 Superamerica. They shared the gigantic tailfins, but were actual runners.

## SPECIFICATION

**YEAR REVEALED** 1955

**PLACE OF ORIGIN** Turin, Italy

**HISTORICAL STATUS** prototype

**ENGINE** none originally fitted but a four-cylinder, 91ci (1,491cc) engine anticipated

**MAXIMUM POWER** unknown

**LAYOUT** front-mounted engine driving the rear wheels

**BODYWORK** two-door, two-seater racer

**TOP SPEED** 140mph (225kph) (notional)

**NUMBER BUILT** one

*"A particularly rich and fortunate year of innumerable projects destined for the other side of the Atlantic."*

GIOVANNI SAVONUZZI, DESIGNER OF THE GILDA, COMMENTING ON THE EVENTS OF 1955

# CITROËN DS

The Citroën DS has an extraordinary mystique—an ability to induce the misty-eyed reverie more normally associated with something genuinely unattainable, such as a Bugatti. That punning French name for the shark-shaped sedan, *Déesse*, means Goddess, and is highly appropriate.

But Citroën actually made just a few less than the proletarian Morris Minor, so it's always been an attainable design icon of the mass-produced age. It was a totally new driving experience, too. The self-leveling suspension system, and its adjustable ride height, ideal for skimming across rutted fields, endowed the DS with serene ride quality. But the power steering, powered front disc brakes, and semi-automatic gearbox were a challenge to master. They all drew their power from the Citroën's central "nervous system" which had dispensed with metal springs for hydro-pneumatic struts. The pin-sharpness of activation this gave—especially in the self-centering steering—felt weird initially, but owners soon grew to love their cars dearly. All that inner wizardry, of course, got technophiles really excited at the DS's 1955 Paris debut. It also heralded an eight-year period during which Citroën's engineers struggled secretly to make the complex DS reliable. To avoid commercial failure, they had to introduce the tamer ID19 version in 1957, with a manual gearbox and non-power steering. It retained all the aerodynamic, futuristic hedonism of the original, but in a format that even a Parisian taxi driver could handle.

## SPECIFICATION

**YEAR REVEALED** 1955

**PLACE OF ORIGIN** Paris, France

**HISTORICAL STATUS**
production car

**ENGINE** four-cylinder, 121–143ci (1,991–2,347cc)

**MAXIMUM POWER** 130bhp

**LAYOUT** front-mounted engine driving the front wheels

**BODYWORK** four-door, five-seater sedan, five-door, five- and seven-station wagon, and two-door, four-seater convertible

**TOP SPEED** 120mph (193kph)

**NUMBER BUILT** 1,456,115

*"This car has had the bravery to be genuine. Unlike the offerings of the American School, it does not seek to woo the buyer with terrible multicolored daubings and plenty of chrome plating, which is a cover-up."*

GIO PONTI, ITALIAN ARCHITECT AND DESIGNER

The DS styling shown in this trio of ID19s photographed in 1957 is still startling even today.

Built by engineer Enrico Nardi to the designs of Carlo Mollino, the Damolnar completed five laps at Le Mans before being blown off-course.

# DAMOLNAR BISILURO

Here's a positive catamaran of a car. The Bisiluro had twin, cigar-shaped "hulls," with the driver seated in the right, and the engine, gearbox, and fuel tank shrouded in the left to balance the weight. Beneath the lower, central portion of the body was a radiator, heat exchanger, and two-stage aerodynamic brake.

The Bisiluro was the brainchild of Carlo Mollino, an architect who loved cars and aircraft. It took shape in the workshops of Enrico Nardi, a Turin-based builder of prototypes and sports cars, in early 1955. Named the Bisiluro—Italian for double torpedo—the "Da-" part of the car's official "marque" alluded to Dr. Mario Damonte,

Giannini badge

the partner in the venture. The whole point of this machine was to tackle the 1955 Le Mans 24-hour race in the 46ci (750cc) class, while gaining the maximum speed advantage from its ground-hugging shape. The power came from a Giannini four-cylinder, 45ci (735cc) unit producing 65bhp at a screaming 6,500rpm—inspired by the engine in Moto Guzzi's racing motorbikes. The Bisiluro was incredibly fast, capable of 133mph (214kph), but on its fifth lap at Le Mans, disaster struck. A Jaguar overtook at such speed that the ensuing gust forced the car off the road, ending its race. Happily, the Bisiluro survived and today resides in Rome's Leonardo da Vinci Science Museum.

## SPECIFICATION

**YEAR REVEALED**  1955

**PLACE OF ORIGIN**  Turin, Italy

**HISTORICAL STATUS**  prototype

**ENGINE**  four-cylinder, 45ci (735cc)

**MAXIMUM POWER**  65bhp

**LAYOUT**  side/mid-mounted engine driving the rear wheels

**BODYWORK**  single-seater racer

**TOP SPEED**  133mph (214kph)

**NUMBER BUILT**  one

*"Absurd and extreme, one of the smallest cars, a twin-boom Nardi, was probably further removed from honest 'prototype' intent than any entry before or since."*

DAVID HODGES IN HIS BOOK *THE LE MANS 24-HOUR RACE*, 1963

This view of the car shows its catamaran configuration to dramatic effect.

The stylish contours of the cars might suggest Detroit but, in fact, this is Vauxhall's production line in Luton, Bedfordshire, UK, in around early 1959. The PA Cresta model, nearest the camera, and the smaller F-type Victors ahead of it brought appealingly sleek American styling and lurid paintwork colours to British and Commonwealth buyers, although the duo later developed a reputation for being rust-prone.

# LINCOLN FUTURA

The iconic Batmobile of the 1966 *Batman* TV series, starring Adam West and Burt Ward, was famously based on a real-life "concept" car: the Lincoln Futura. Designed at Ford, and built in Italy in 1955 by Ghia for a reputed $250,000, it was driven through New York on May 3 that year by Benson Ford, Henry Ford's grandson.

Repainted red from its original pearlescent light blue, the Futura then starred alongside Debbie Reynolds and Glenn Ford in the 1959 MGM movie *It Started With A Kiss*. Afterward, it was acquired by leading Hollywood custom-car king George Barris, who fancied the Futura—with those gigantic tailfins and sinister hooded headlights—might come in handy. He was right: in 1965, ABC asked Barris to create a dramatic car for its TV incarnation of DC Comics' superhero Batman. With just three weeks to complete the job, Barris realized his Futura was already halfway there. He kept the chassis, Ford V8 engine, and basic profile unaltered, while artfully modifying the nose section to resemble a bat-like facemask. He then extended the leading edges of the Futura's already huge fins to evoke bat wings, and scalloped their trailing edges for an even more swooping effect. The concealed wheelarches were opened up, and the car's color changed to black, with fluorescent red highlights. The original car has remained in Barris's ownership. The Futura ultimately achieved immortality by establishing the style for all Batmobiles since: long, dark, and powerful.

## SPECIFICATION

**YEAR REVEALED** 1955

**PLACE OF ORIGIN** Detroit, Michigan, and Turin, Italy

**HISTORICAL STATUS** prototype

**ENGINE** V8-cylinder, 390ci (6,384cc)

**MAXIMUM POWER** unknown

**LAYOUT** front-mounted engine driving the rear wheels

**BODYWORK** two-door, two-seater roadster

**TOP SPEED** unknown

**NUMBER BUILT** one

*"Atomic batteries to power. Turbines to speed."*

BURT WARD AS ROBIN IN *BATMAN*, 1966

The original Lincoln Futura as envisaged by Ford's designers and Ghia's craftsmen.

The Batmobile, created by custom car guru George Barris, here with Adam West in its final TV incarnation in 1979.

The backers of the 1956 Powerdrive did everything they could to make it appear a "real" roadster rather than a puny penny-pincher.

# POWERDRIVE

In the arcane world of British microcars, David Gottlieb is a near-mythical figure. The designer of three of the most infamous of these Suez crisis-era fuel-misers—the Allard Clipper, Powerdrive, and the Coronet—the whiff of failure surrounding them is also the aroma of his mystique.

In 1953, Gottlieb's Powerdrive company sold the concept of a three-wheeled economy car with rear-mounted, single-cylinder engine and egg-shaped fiberglass body to London sports car manufacturer Sydney Allard. The car had serious design flaws, especially overheating, and Allard bailed out in June 1955 after making just 22. Yet, an undaunted Gottlieb launched his own Powerdrive car just a month later, this time backed by London garage chain Blue Star.

It was a small, aluminum-bodied sports car with three-abreast seating and attractive lines. It had two wheels at the front with a single, rear wheel cleverly concealed by the supposed "big car" styling. Gottlieb thought buyers wanted a stylish car that hid its austerity because, weighing under 0.4 tons, it attracted motorcycle tax rates. The tubular chassis had a two-stroke British Anzani motorbike engine forward of the rear wheel, with a three-speed-and-reverse Albion gearbox, and Austin A30 steering and front suspension. Talk of selling five a week, however, proved hopelessly optimistic. At £412, a "real" car such as the Ford Popular cost just £1 more. But two years later, Gottlieb recreated the car as the Coronet— which proved his motor industry swansong.

## SPECIFICATION

**YEAR REVEALED**  1956

**PLACE OF ORIGIN**  London, UK

**HISTORICAL STATUS**
production car

**ENGINE**  two-cylinder, 20ci (322cc)

**MAXIMUM POWER**  15bhp

**LAYOUT**  rear-mounted engine
driving the rear wheel

**BODYWORK**  two-door,
two-seater roadster

**TOP SPEED**  60mph (97kph)

**NUMBER BUILT**  unknown

*"Look closely and you'll see it's a three-wheeler cleverly disguised to look like a grown-up four-wheeler."*

DAILY EXPRESS NEWSPAPER, 1956

One luggage compartment was at the back, beside the tiny engine, and another upfront.

The gold-painted Golden Rocket was a big pull at General Motors's 1956 Motorama traveling show.

# OLDSMOBILE GOLDEN ROCKET

One of the stars of General Motors's 1956 Motorama line-up, this space-age dream car certainly added sparkle to Oldsmobile's dowdy image. Its interior, too, boasted clever ideas that made for easy access despite a very snug, close-coupled cockpit.

When the driver or passenger door was opened, a roof panel would automatically swing upwards. Simultaneously, the seat would rise by 3in (8cm) and swivel round 45 degrees to accept the occupant. Once enclosed, the driver was then faced with an incredible steering wheel. A thin rim was supported by two spokes that formed, de facto, the steering column, tapering right back into the dashboard to converge with the distant steering wheel "center," which was actually a large speedometer. Buttons on the wheel meant it could be tilted to suit the driver, or make access even easier—a genuine innovation. The rocket-inspired exterior suggested ultra-rapid forward acceleration. Positively glowing in its burnished gold paintwork, the plastic body featured prominent chrome warheads fronting each wing, which then tapered gently to two chrome tips. The effect was like two torpedoes, enlivened with two small fins at the rear that looked something of an afterthought. Among its 1956 Motorama stablemates on their pan-US tour, the Golden Rocket was eye-catching; on its own, it was sensational. When it was exhibited solo at the Paris motor show 18 months after its American unveiling, it was still acclaimed as one of the absolute stars of the show.

## SPECIFICATION

**YEAR REVEALED** 1956

**PLACE OF ORIGIN** Detroit, Michigan

**HISTORICAL STATUS** prototype

**ENGINE** V8-cylinder, 371ci (6,079cc)

**MAXIMUM POWER** 275bhp

**LAYOUT** front-mounted engine driving the rear wheels

**BODYWORK** two-door, two-seater coupé

**TOP SPEED** unknown

**NUMBER BUILT** one

*"The Motorama years put a tremendous strain on everyone because every studio had to work nights and weekends on dream cars."*

TOM CHRISTIANSEN, GM DESIGNER, IN *A CENTURY OF AUTOMOTIVE STYLE* BY MICHAEL LAMM AND DAVE HOLLS, 1997

# PONTIAC XP-200 CLUB DE MER

After all the space-age excess that had characterized the so-called "dream cars" paraded by General Motors in the first half of the 1950s, the Club De Mer was as refreshing as a sea breeze.

Not that it wasn't a dramatic-looking car, especially with its prominent stabilizing dorsal fin jutting out from the rear deck. But rather than trying to apply the rather inappropriate imagery from jet aircraft and space rockets to car proportions, the design team, led by chief Harley Earl and Pontiac studio leader Paul Gillian, turned to land speed record cars. By their very nature, the forms of these cars was defined by their function. In much the same way, the Club De Mer was a two-seater roadster whose low ground-hugging stance gave the impression of a purposeful body tightly wrapped around the powerful mechanical elements and cockpit. Its low frontal area, concealed headlights, and overall smoothness were enlivened by a pair of chrome "silver streaks" running from the nosecone to the hood air scoops. In typical 1950s GM fashion, the Club De Mer did a tour of duty as part of the 1956 Motorama show. It was also immortalized for kids as a best-selling Revell plastic model.

## SPECIFICATION

**YEAR REVEALED** 1956

**PLACE OF ORIGIN** Detroit, Michigan

**HISTORICAL STATUS** prototype

**ENGINE** V8-cylinder, 268ci (4,392cc)

**MAXIMUM POWER** 300bhp

**LAYOUT** front-mounted engine driving the rear wheels

**BODYWORK** two-door, two-seater roadster

**TOP SPEED** unknown

**NUMBER BUILT** one

*"The Pontiac Club De Mer was a metaphor for America in mid-decade: the name and details evoke a cosmopolitanism that was superficially attractive but ultimately colorless."*

STEPHEN BAYLEY IN HIS BOOK *HARLEY EARL*, 1990

Pontiac's Club De Mer was sleek from any angle, yet it was very purposeful by contemporary "dream car" standards.

# RENAULT ETOILE FILANTE

The two buzz phrases in the global car industry of the 1950s were "aerodynamics" and "jet-powered." Many show cars of the time adopted one of these themes to grab attention, but Renault decided to unite both in 1956, to pursue a serious goal: the world land speed record for a gas-turbine car. The intention was to study "problems of control, roadholding, and braking far in excess of their present knowledge" and, more usefully, to sprinkle a little marketing gold-dust on the new Renault Dauphine family car.

One of France's most experienced race car designers, Albert Lory, was summoned to help build the car, which was called *Etoile Filante* (or "Shooting Star"). It was never intended for actual racing, although with Lory's experience it naturally adopted a spaceframe design, plastic body, enormous disc brakes, and Porsche-type torsion bar suspension. The rear-mounted gas turbine power unit, called Turmo 1, came from French aero engine maker Turboméca. Any driver must have felt mild apprehension with three fuel tanks on board, including a synthetic rubber bag-type one in the car's low-slung nose. The car was freighted to the Bonneville Salt Flats in Utah for its speed record attempt. Hand-picked test driver Jean Hebert achieved 191.2mph (307.7kph), snatching the speed record for turbine cars from Rover. The dilapidated car was finally renovated by Renault in the 1990s and, for the first time since 1956, ran again under its own power.

## SPECIFICATION

**YEAR REVEALED** 1956

**PLACE OF ORIGIN** Paris, France

**HISTORICAL STATUS** speed record car

**ENGINE** gas turbine

**MAXIMUM POWER** 270bhp

**LAYOUT** rear-mounted engine driving the rear wheels

**BODYWORK** single-seater racer

**TOP SPEED** 191mph (307kph)

**NUMBER BUILT** one

*"The results already achieved give promise that one day the motorist will be able to acquire turbine cars of simple design which will be easy to drive, reasonably priced, and economical to maintain."* AUTOMOBILE YEAR, AN ANNUAL YEARBOOK, 1957

France was a latecomer to the gas turbine car arena, but the Etoile Filante did at least deliver on Renault's attempt at a speed record.

Visitors thronging the 1952 Geneva Salon;
the event continues today as one of the
very few annual car shows (most are
biennial). Because of Switzerland's
economic importance—and perhaps
because of the lack of a motor industry of
its own—the salon has unique standing in
the automotive industry. Hence, the many
American cars on display here, a rarity in
Europe then as it is now.

# AURORA

The Aurora wasn't quite the first experimental "safety" car. That accolade goes to "Survival Car 1", revealed in 1957, and bankrolled by the Liberty Mutual insurance company.

Aurora was unveiled the same year but, in contrast, was fully-functioning (rather than a static exhibit). More importantly, the Aurora took careful account of pedestrian safety. This remarkable-looking car was the four-year project of a Catholic priest, Father Alfred Juliano of the Order of the Holy Ghost, with financial help from his congregation. His safety-first outlook led him to include seatbelts, side-impact bars, a collapsible telescopic steering column, and a curved, deeply-padded dashboard free of sharp projections. The seats could be swiveled around in the face of an impending, unavoidable accident. The Aurora's tinted "Astrodome" roof had three thick, built-in roll-over protection bars. Reporters roasted the car's unveiling at Manhattan's Hotel New Yorker, but entirely missed the point because the bizarre plastic contours, with wheels, radiator grille, and lights tucked deep away, were meant to stop a pedestrian from sustaining injury in just about any accidental contact. At a tentative US$12,000, it was almost as costly as the top Cadillac of the era; Father Juliano didn't receive a single order, despite offering a choice of power units. He was later forced to leave his church after allegations of misappropriating parishioners' cash and personal bankruptcy.

## SPECIFICATION

**YEAR REVEALED** 1957

**PLACE OF ORIGIN** Branford, Connecticut

**HISTORICAL STATUS** prototype

**ENGINE** V8-cylinder, 322ci (5,272cc)

**MAXIMUM POWER** 166bhp

**LAYOUT** front-mounted engine driving the rear wheels

**BODYWORK** four-door, four-seater sedan

**TOP SPEED** unknown

**NUMBER BUILT** one

*"Despite having no mechanical knowledge, Father Juliano set out to put his heart and soul into that car. I think the whole story is so sad. He died a broken man, because he lost his dream."*

ANDY SAUNDERS, PRESENT OWNER AND RESTORER OF THE AURORA, NEW YORK TIMES, 2007

Father Alfred Juliano at the wheel of his Aurora car, developed with the object of maximizing safety for both occupants and pedestrians.

The upright grille was distinctive, but the 1958 Edsel range, including this Pacer, was shunned; buyers surmised that the cars offered little of merit.

# EDSEL PACER

Edsel was an exercise in corporate buccaneering that rapidly became a byword for failure. The venture proved an expensive fiasco for Ford (it lost $350 million), and the resultant cars were extraordinary for their very ordinariness.

The idea for the brand came from Ford's conclusion that it was being outpaced by arch-rival General Motors and its five US marques. Ford decided to install another division between the basic Ford range and the sports-luxury Mercury. In 1955, it hired poet Marianne Moore for her linguistic expertise to find a new name for it. "Intelligent Whale" and "Utopian Turtletop" were both mooted before the new company section was called Edsel, after Henry Ford's late son.

Early ideas for a completely new car were abandoned on cost grounds, and a cocktail of existing engines, driveline, and bodywork was assembled—Ford parts for the cheaper Pacer/Ranger range, Mercury components for the pricier Citation/Corsair. Distinctive Edsel touches included a vertical front grille shaped like a horse collar, and a "Teletouch" push-button gearchange in the steering wheel. Launched in a TV spectacular hosted by Bing Crosby, the 13-car range sold sluggishly from the start. The break-even sales point was 650 cars daily, but averaged about 300. The reasons were complex: sales of large, thirsty cars like Edsels were decimated by imports and compact models; quality was mediocre; Ford dealer support half-hearted; and the public underwhelmed.

## SPECIFICATION

**YEAR REVEALED** 1957

**PLACE OF ORIGIN** Detroit, Michigan

**HISTORICAL STATUS** production car

**ENGINE** V8-cylinder, 361ci (5,915cc)

**MAXIMUM POWER** 304bhp

**LAYOUT** front-mounted engine driving the rear wheels

**BODYWORK** five-seater sedan and four-seater convertible

**TOP SPEED** 105mph (169kph)

**NUMBER BUILT** 19,057

> *"Edsel—it's a great car!"*
>
> FRANK SINATRA, A GUEST ON *THE EDSEL SHOW*, OCTOBER 13, 1957

THIS IS THE EDSEL
*never before a car like it*

*newest expression of fine engineering from Ford Motor Company*

Edsel marketing was persuasive, although the irony here was of course unintentional.

# FIAT NUOVA 500

Despite Fiat's 1936 500 "Topolino" being a well-liked little car in its day, the Nuova 500 of 1957 is what the motoring world today perceives as the original 500. The first 500 had a tiny four-cylinder engine, water-cooled and front-mounted; this all-new one boasted a twin-cylinder, air-cooled powerpack at the back.

Intended as utilitarian transportation for the masses, it was brought to the market by Fiat in response to an Italian government pledge to boost car ownership by investing heavily in Italy's main road and highway network. The man in charge of development was Fiat's Dante Giacosa, also the genius behind the original 500 during a 50-year career with the company. The Nuova 500 was meant to get cash-strapped Italians off their scooters, but it still offered fresh air: until 1966 every 500 came with a full-length sunroof. A toy-like four-seater with go-kart handling, the original cars were "powered" by a 29ci (479cc) twin offering a paltry 13bhp, mercifully lifted to 30ci (499cc) and 18bhp for the 500D in 1960 so it could cruise at 55mph (89kph). Buyers were just as sold on the 50mpg (18km/l) fuel economy. Early cars had rear-hinged "suicide" doors, but post-1965 500F models gained conventional front hinges. The 500L version of 1968 offered buyers luxury via the three simple additions of carpets, reclining seats, and chrome bumpers.

## SPECIFICATION

**YEAR REVEALED**  1957

**PLACE OF ORIGIN**  Turin, Italy

**HISTORICAL STATUS**
production car

**ENGINE**  two-cylinder, 29–36ci (479–594cc)

**MAXIMUM POWER**  23bhp

**LAYOUT**  rear-mounted engine driving the rear wheels

**BODYWORK**  two-door, four-seater sedan and estate

**TOP SPEED**  60mph (97kph)

**NUMBER BUILT**  3,408,036

*"An impressive feature of the car is its roadholding. A driver imagines it would roll excessively when cornering. But he is quickly reassured that it does not."*

THE AUTOCAR MAGAZINE ROAD TEST, 1957

A Fiat advertisement reflecting the instant affection Italy held for the Nuova 500.

Early examples offered a full-length convertible roof while retaining fixed screen pillars and side windows, boosting the car's "fun" factor.

# COOPER T43/45 CLIMAX

Formula One racing was changed forever by this car, after its first Grand Prix win in Argentina in 1958. Stirling Moss joined the private Rob Walker team to drive a strange little rear-engined car that even the event organizers were reluctant to let take part.

The tiny, dark blue machine was so light compared to its front-engined rivals—partly due to a chassis incorporating unconventional curved links—that it didn't need to stop for tire changes. That, allied to Moss's superlative driving, meant he eventually passed everyone, including Fangio and Hawthorn in their Ferraris, to swipe victory. During the following three years, Cooper T45s and T51s—using 122, 134, and 153ci (2,000, 2,200, and then 2,500cc) Coventry Climax engines—twice brought

the tiny British company the Constructors's World Championship. The front-engined Formula One car was rendered utterly obsolete. Mid-engined machines had competed in the 1930s and, while formidable, they were hard work to drive with their enormous power and weight, and narrow tires. The Cooper Car Company began by building motorbike-engined racing cars for Formula 500. As this evolved into Formula Three, Coopers developed in parallel, and by 1957 the cars were Formula Two regulars. After Moss's stunning win in Buenos Aires, Australia's Jack Brabham twice became World Champion driving for Cooper in 1959 and 1960. By 1961, every car on the Formula One grid had adopted the Cooper's layout—Ferrari included.

## SPECIFICATION

**YEAR REVEALED** 1958

**PLACE OF ORIGIN** Surbiton, Surrey, UK

**HISTORICAL STATUS** Formula One racing car

**ENGINE** four-cylinder, 120–152ci (1,960–2,495cc)

**MAXIMUM POWER** 240bhp

**LAYOUT** rear-mounted engine driving the rear wheels

**BODYWORK** single-seater racer

**TOP SPEED** 140mph+ (225kph+)

**NUMBER BUILT** 30/26

*"When we came to make our first 500cc racer, it was just a hell of a lot more convenient to have the engine at the back, driving a chain. We certainly had no feeling that we were creating some scientific breakthrough!"*

JOHN COOPER, IN *JOHN COOPER: A VERY BRITISH MARQUE, A VERY BRITISH MAN* BY DAVID TREMAYNE, 2001

The Formula One establishment was caught napping by the tiny British Cooper outfit with its hugely influential rear-engined cars.

# TRABANT

The collapse of the Berlin Wall in 1989 was the most symbolic event in the ending of the "Cold War" between East and West. But the emergence of the Trabant, spluttering its way into a bright new Europe, was the automotive equivalent. West German motorists were horrified at its highly polluting, two-stroke 600cc (37ci) engine, basic safety systems, and body panels made from rubbish—resin-strengthened wood pulp and cotton. But that is what East German drivers had cheerfully endured since 1958, when the first "Trabbi" went on sale as the only small car for the country's citizens.

Weirdly, for a car known successively as the Trabant (for "Traveler") P50, P60, and P601, the hood badge was a prominent "S". It was a legacy of the East German government's motor industry nationalization policy. After the eastern territory was annexed in 1945, the former Audi and Horch factories found themselves locked behind the "Iron Curtain," and in 1958 they were merged to form VEB Sachsenring Automobilwerke. Sachsenring was the name of a nearby racing circuit, hence the "S" on the Trabant. Little changed on the Trabant during its 33 years: a station wagon came in 1960; a bigger engine in 1963; a further power hike in 1969 to 26bhp; and coil spring suspension to replace its antediluvian swing axles in 1988. After German reunification in 1990, a modern VW Polo engine and front disc brakes were added. Production ended in 1991, but few former East Germans were sad to see it smoking off into the sunset.

## SPECIFICATION

**YEAR REVEALED** 1958

**PLACE OF ORIGIN** Zwickau, former East Germany

**HISTORICAL STATUS** production car

**ENGINE** two-cylinder, 31–36ci (500–595cc)

**MAXIMUM POWER** 25bhp

**LAYOUT** front-mounted engine driving the front wheels

**BODYWORK** two-door, four-seater sedan, estate, and open utility

**TOP SPEED** 62mph (100kph)

**NUMBER BUILT** 3,096,000

*"East German small car users make do with this modest little runabout, which has a Duroplast plastic body on a steel platform"*

DAILY EXPRESS GUIDE TO WORLD CARS, 1987

A Trabant P601 Tourist: this one dates from around 1980, but it's virtually identical to the 1960 original.

The hulk of the Zil 111 limousine was not something to be savored in the rear-view mirror of the 1950s Russian roadscape.

# ZIL 111

Who would have guessed that the brutal communist dictator Joseph Stalin had a secret, and decadent, car passion—he loved large American Packard limousines. In fact, he loved the traditional majesty of the Packard Super Eight so much that he ordered the country's premier truckmaker, ZIS, to manufacture a close copy that would then be used as official transport for government ministers, other dignitaries, and official parade car duties. Thus, until 1958, the country's top car, the ZIS 110, was a regal, but increasingly dated, behemoth.

Stalin died in 1953, and three years later so did Ivan Likhachev. Little known internationally, Likhachev had been the director of the ZIS plant in Moscow, and was held in such esteem that the factory was renamed ZIL in his honor. The program to replace the ZIS 110 was well underway, and the new car was finally revealed in 1958. The Russians might have been proud of their chrome-laden Z1L 111 but, to western eyes, it was already behind the times, resembling a Packard Patrician frontage grafted on to a Chrysler Crown Imperial body. At 65in (164cm), it was taller than the American cars it imitated, and was extremely heavy, needing a 365ci (5,980cc) V8 engine and automatic transmission to haul it along. This sinister car was luxuriously appointed within, with leather seats, air conditioning, and electric windows. The sight of ZIL 111s thundering along their dedicated lane on Russian highways must have inspired amazement among the average citizen.

## SPECIFICATION

**YEAR REVEALED** 1958

**PLACE OF ORIGIN** Moscow, Russia

**HISTORICAL STATUS** production car

**ENGINE** V8-cylinder, 365ci (5,980cc)

**MAXIMUM POWER** 220bhp

**LAYOUT** front-mounted engine driving the rear wheels

**BODYWORK** four-door, seven-seater limousine

**TOP SPEED** 96mph (154kph)

**NUMBER BUILT** 112

*"The ZIL design team were under pressure from the Kremlin to out-do American designs."*

ANDY THOMPSON, IN HIS BOOK *CARS OF THE SOVIET UNION*, 2008

This fantastic vista is "Suburbia in the 21st century," as predicted by designers working at Ford's Advanced Styling Studio in 1957. "Tomorrow's typical commuter scene." they declared, "will still find mother and the children waiting at the station for father to come home from the office." They were right about the daily drudge, if sadly off-target in the utopian streamlined look of the monorail future.

The Ghia Selene I grew from studies for an extreme rear-engined Renault and then vanished in Moscow while being "evaluated" as a taxi.

# GHIA SELENE

These two remarkable, rear-engined design studies put the steering wheel, driver, and front passenger forward of the front wheels, and the engine protruding in its own rear compartment. It was "two box" thinking, only in reverse.

The Selene I grew out of a Ghia design program for Renault, itself a champion of rear-engined cars. Unlike the ugly Renault 900 study, though, the Ghia Selene would be startlingly futuristic—oozing the jet-age imagery characteristic of many 1950s Ghia show cars, and with an engine at the extreme back like some contemporary airliners. The work of young stylist Tom Tjaarda, a most astonishing feature was a steering wheel that could switch from left- to right-hand drive, with two sets of pedals permanently in position on the floor. In the rear compartment, two pairs of seats faced each other, with a built-in cocktail bar for mobile "relaxation." The car was meant to predict an age of superhighways, where electronic controls did the navigation work and car occupants sailed along in serene comfort. Nevertheless, this didn't take into account the undoubted vulnerability the Selene driver would feel, pushed out so far in front. Ghia built its gleaming white Selene II in 1960, along similar lines but a three-seater—a single driving seat and two facing seats, and an built-in TV, in the back. This time, the shape was executed by American Virgil Exner Junior, whose father oversaw design at Ghia client Chrysler; it was even more way-out, sportier, and even less practical.

> ## SPECIFICATION
>
> **YEAR REVEALED** 1959
>
> **PLACE OF ORIGIN** Turin, Italy
>
> **HISTORICAL STATUS** prototype
>
> **ENGINE** none fitted, but said to be suitable for engines from 61–153ci (1,000-2,500cc)
>
> **MAXIMUM POWER** unknown
>
> **LAYOUT** rear-mounted engine driving the rear wheels
>
> **BODYWORK** four-door, five-seater sedan and canopy entry/single-door, three-seater coupé
>
> **TOP SPEED** unknown
>
> **NUMBER BUILT** two

*"It might fly if it had wings—or an engine. Two back seats, facing each other, give the back compartment a lounge-room effect, complete with bar."*

MODERN MECHANIX MAGAZINE, 1960

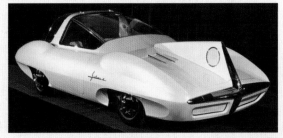

Selene II was also rear-biased but with the extra futuristic frisson of on-board TV.

The Mini's long period on sale made anniversaries routine: this is the 1989 Mini 30 (left) with the Mini Cooper that won the 1964 Monte Carlo Rally.

# BMC MINI

The Mini provided cheap transport, technical brilliance, motor sport dominance, and classless style. It's also Britain's best-ever selling car.

It was conceived by one man, Alec Issigonis, a gifted engineer hired by the British Motor Corporation in 1956. Almost immediately, the Suez crisis emerged, forcing gas rationing on British motorists, and creating an urgent need for up-to-date economy cars. Issigonis envisaged a highly-compact "cube," in which the four passengers would sit, headed by a space-saving front-wheel drive system. Issigonis's imagination overcame the small dimensions by mounting the gearbox under the engine instead of behind it, and specifying a compact rubber cone suspension system.

Packaging was the 10ft- (3m-) long Mini's greatest strength. The interior was staggeringly roomy. Every square inch was used: there were big door bins for storage; a parcel shelf instead of a dashboard; and tiny, space-saving 10in (25cm) wheels. Launched on August 26, 1959, as the Austin Mini Seven and Morris Mini-Minor, the £496 starting price made it virtually the cheapest car on sale. Buyers adored the Mini for its thrift and its verve. Its tenacious road grip meant it ran rings around expensive sports cars, it was easy to park, and it looked chic. There were numerous updates during its 41-year life, but the investment needed to build it meant that, for years, it sold at a loss, adding to the rocky fortunes of BMC and its successors.

## SPECIFICATION

**YEAR REVEALED** 1959

**PLACE OF ORIGIN** Birmingham, West Midlands, UK

**HISTORICAL STATUS** production car

**ENGINE** four-cylinder, 52–78ci (848–1,275cc)

**MAXIMUM POWER** 76bhp

**LAYOUT** front-mounted engine driving the front wheels

**BODYWORK** two-door, four-seater sedan and station wagon

**TOP SPEED** 100mph (161kph)

**NUMBER BUILT** 5,387,862

*"Don't expect me to be modest about the Mini. I'm very proud that it has run for so long and it still looks like the car we designed."*

SIR ALEC ISSIGONIS, FATHER OF THE MINI

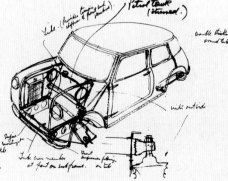

One of Alec Issigonis's famous back-of-envelope sketches for the Mini's brilliant concept.

# SHAMROCK

Ireland has few car-making boasts, despite Henry Ford's establishment of a Model T assembly plant in Cork as early as 1917. But the Shamrock is a rare exception, built with the ambition of captivating US customers.

Possibly inspired by the American success of the Nash Metropolitan, Californian businessman Wilbur Curtis decided to up the style stakes by selling a shrunken copy of the contemporary Ford Thunderbird, yet powered by the same Austin 92ci (1,500cc) engine found under the Metropolitan's two-tone steelwork. And he'd make sure it had that desirable "import" aura by building it in Europe. He chose Tralee in County Kerry, Ireland. The fiberglass-bodied car came together, with help from Canadian race driver Alvin "Spike" Rhiando, around a simple ladder-frame chassis with almost every mechanical component taken from the Austin A55. As a European-size car, it looked overbodied on its 98in (2.5m) wheelbase, with huge front and rear overhangs, and a narrow track. However, unlike the Metropolitan, it was a full four-seater convertible, with optional removable hardtop. Production only started after a move to Castleblaney, County Monaghan, and Curtis was bullish, anticipating 3,000 sales in 1960 and 10,000 annually thereafter. No doubt underfinancing scuppered the plans, though, together with several serious design flaws. Reports vary, but no more than ten were made in six months, and the remaining stock of spares was rumored to have been dumped in a local Loch. Four survive today.

## SPECIFICATION

**YEAR REVEALED** 1959

**PLACE OF ORIGIN** Castleblaney, County Monaghan, Ireland

**HISTORICAL STATUS** production car

**ENGINE** four-cylinder, 91ci (1,489cc)

**MAXIMUM POWER** 53bhp

**LAYOUT** front-mounted engine driving the rear wheels

**BODYWORK** two-door, four-seater convertible

**TOP SPEED** 90mph (145kph) (claimed)

**NUMBER BUILT** approximately ten

The cover of a rare Shamrock brochure, highlighting Ireland's lush greenery.

*"The Irish T-Bird at half the price, reports* Motor Trend; *special design reinforced fiberglass resin body. Top-rated speed 90mph—an honest 38mpg economy."*

FROM A SALES LEAFLET FOR THE SHAMROCK, 1960

Spurred on by the success of the Nash Metropolitan, the Anglo-Irish Shamrock aimed to conquer US hearts yet proved an utter flop.

It might not come as a surprise to learn that the gadget-laden specification of the Fulgur was inspired by suggestions from French comic-readers.

# SIMCA FULGUR

The Simca Fulgur (*fulgur* is Latin for "flash") is possibly the silliest concept car of the 1950s. But that wasn't surprising—the project was a fantasy car of the year 2000, created with suggestions from young readers of a French children's magazine.

Had it ever worked as the children intended, it would have been electrically driven, taking its power from a live rail buried in the road surface. When the Fulgur's speed reached 90mph (145kph), its two front wheels would retract into the body so that it would, somehow, plane along on its rear two wheels, steered by rudders. Fortunately, however, an on-board gyroscope would make sure the car tracked upright and stably. A fiendish combination of radar and a computer, or "electronic brain" as Simca preferred to call it, would look after navigation. And it had the obligatory 1950s dream car feature: a huge tailfin (in this case V-shaped). Although there were doubts about how all this untried technology would actually function, the Fulgur went down a storm at the 1959 Geneva Motor Show, and was still a crowd-puller when it appeared at the Chicago Auto Show in 1961. The most significant thing about the Fulgur was the man who designed the static mock-up, 27-year-old architect Robert Opron. Although he was made redundant from Simca's styling department in 1961 (spending two years designing fridges and stoves), he returned to the car industry and was responsible for the acclaimed looks of the Citroen SM and the Renault Fuego.

## SPECIFICATION

**YEAR REVEALED** 1959

**PLACE OF ORIGIN** Paris, France

**HISTORICAL STATUS** prototype

**ENGINE** none fitted, but intended for an electric engine

**MAXIMUM POWER** unknown

**LAYOUT** rear-mounted engine driving the rear wheels

**BODYWORK** canopy-entry, two-seater coupé

**TOP SPEED** unknown

**NUMBER BUILT** one

*"It was a fun job. It was the sort of job you gave to the office youngster—but when they [Simca] saw that it made quite an impact with the public, they started to make use of it."*

ROBERT OPRON, THE FULGUR'S DESIGNER, IN *CLASSIC & SPORTS CAR* MAGAZINE

# STEYR-PUCH HAFLINGER

A specific little vehicle intended for specific uses, the Haflinger was created with scant regard for passenger niceties and a total focus on off-road ability. Although many were built as pickups and military field cars, some came as open four-seaters, qualifying them as "automobiles."

The Haflinger was a tiny four-wheel drive contraption powered by Steyr's flat-twin engine from an Austrian-made version of the Fiat Nuova 500. It was extremely trim—light enough to be lifted and carried by four people—yet could also carry a 0.5-ton payload, which endeared it greatly to Alpine hill farmers. Ingeniously simple, yet stark in appearance, in action it clattered its way up 50-degree slopes with gusto, and scattered mud as it bounced across soggy farmland.

Several aspects aided its exceptional off-road ability. Front and rear differential locks kept it moving in the stickiest of terrain, while high-ground clearance was provided by swing axles back and front to keep the axle center higher than the wheel hubs. Similarities to pre-war Tatras were no accident: the Haflinger's designer Erich Ledwinka was the son of Tatra engineer Hans Ledwinka.

It was largely unaltered between 1959 and the end of manufacture in 1974, when Steyr replaced it with a similar, but much larger vehicle: the Pinzgauer. As a staple in military fleets around the world, it's still made today, albeit now by BAE Systems in the UK. Haflinger and Pinzgauer, incidentally are both breeds of horse.

## SPECIFICATION

**YEAR REVEALED** 1959

**PLACE OF ORIGIN** Graz, Austria

**HISTORICAL STATUS**
production car

**ENGINE** two-cylinder, 39ci (643cc)

**MAXIMUM POWER** 28bhp

**LAYOUT** rear-mounted engine
driving all four wheels

**BODYWORK** door-less four-seater
convertible/utility

**TOP SPEED** 40mph (64kph)

**NUMBER BUILT** 16,647

*"It retains a cult following among hairshirt hippies and hardcore Hebridean farmers alike. If only Frodo had had one, the* Lord Of The Rings *would have been a novella."*

MICHAEL BOOTH, *INDEPENDENT ON SUNDAY* NEWSPAPER, 2005

With an optional rear seat, the four-wheel drive Haflinger—beloved of Alpine farmers—just about qualifies as a car.

# 4

## 1960–1969

# A DECADE WITHOUT LIMITS

The emancipation of youth, the white heat of technology, the dawn of the classless culture—there are many phrases that could sum up the 1960s and the whole galaxy of exciting automobiles that were generated during the decade.

For one thing, clever new types of engine really did hit the road for the first time. These included innovations such as the rotary and the gas turbine engines. There were developments in car body design and layout too, with sport-utility vehicles and hatchbacks changing the way cars were driven and used.

A shift in thinking in drivelines also brought high-technology front- and four-wheel drive configurations, and these proliferated in everything from small city cars to sporting racers. And for the first time there was a proper, scientific focus on making cars safer, to the lasting benefit of all road users.

The 1960s also saw automobiles develop a following of their own as exciting elements in movies and TV shows—it may have taken more than 70 years, but popular culture on wheels had finally arrived.

With its wheels arranged in a rhomboid configuration, the X is one of the strangest-looking sedans that designers have ever come up with.

# PININFARINA X

Car designers had explored just about every wheel configuration by the dawn of the 1960s. These even included wheels arranged in a diamond pattern, both as a shortlived production car, a Sunbeam, and several prototypes, the Vannod, the Voisin, and the Gordon. Pininfarina's X, though, pushed the parameters out further by using a rhomboid for the car's "footprint."

This amazing four-door sedan had, in effect, two wheelbases—one from the single front wheel to the two in the center, and one from the center wheels to the rear wheel.

The smoothly pointed nose had the car's only steered wheel hidden deep in its center, and was fronted by three headlights beneath a Plexiglass fairing with three prominent chrome overriders beneath for protection.

At the back, the single powered wheel was similarly concealed and the tail, housing the 66ci (1,089cc) Fiat engine, was dominated by its twin stabilizing, buttress-type fins.

Pininfarina was happy to build the car as a display showpiece for the Turin motor show, but for Alberto Morelli of the Turin Polytechnic, it was a serious study of aerodynamics and fuel economy, exploiting some of his design patents.

Pininfarina still has the car in its collection although not in the same form as it originated in fall 1960. The rear doors that hinged from the back were changed to front-hinged types before road testing. The X also led to Y, a Pininfarina city car prototype, similar in profile but with wheels back to their four-cornered convention.

## SPECIFICATION

**YEAR REVEALED**  1960

**PLACE OF ORIGIN**  Turin, Italy

**HISTORICAL STATUS**  prototype

**ENGINE**  four-cylinder, 66ci (1,089cc)

**MAXIMUM POWER**  43bhp

**LAYOUT**  rear-mounted engine driving the rearmost wheel

**BODYWORK**  four-door, four-seater sedan

**TOP SPEED**  90mph (145kph)

**NUMBER BUILT**  one

*"Most revolutionary vision on four wheels: one for driving, one steering, two stabilizers... Pininfarina was the first designer to marry together form and function, then send them off on their honeymoon as a harmonious whole."*

GERRY BUTCHER, *DAILY MAIL* NEWSPAPER, 1966

# AMPHICAR 770

The Amphicar is the only amphibious car to reach proper mass-production. As a plaything for rivers and calm lakes it was enormous fun. But for anything more seagoing it was a precarious hazard, as shown in 1965 by a revealing report in *Autocar* magazine.

Two Amphicars attempted to cross the English Channel. One broke down after letting in too much water and the second had to tow it, after disentangling the towrope from its propellers. When the overworked car's puny 12-gallon (45-liter) fuel tank was empty, it had to be refilled. "A rather precarious operation," the report noted, "which involved opening the roof and pouring the fuel into the tank from over the windscreen".

No doubt the German manufacturer didn't advocate this type of journey, but the cars did finally reach land. They were aimed primarily at rich outdoorsmen in the US, where 80 percent of Amphicars were sold.

The car was designed by German engineer Hans Trippel. It had a 70ci (1,147cc) Triumph Herald engine, a two-part transmission with an adapted VW Beetle gearbox for the road, and a two-speed (forward-and-back) in-water unit. The wheels and the twin propellers could operate independently and the steering wheel controlled the rudders – the front wheels.

Manufacture stopped in 1963 after over-ambitious forecasts produced a huge inventory of parts. Amphicars were then built from the remaining stock until 1968.

## SPECIFICATION

**YEAR REVEALED** 1961

**PLACE OF ORIGIN** Berlin, West Germany

**HISTORICAL STATUS** production car

**ENGINE** four-cylinder, 70ci (1,147 cc)

**MAXIMUM POWER** 43bhp

**LAYOUT** rear-mounted engine driving the rear wheels

**BODYWORK** four-seater convertible

**TOP SPEED** 70mph (112kph) on land; 7mph (12kph) in water

**NUMBER BUILT** 3,878

*"It was found better to motor up the wave with the accelerator full down, and when the top of the wave was reached to slacken off and gently motor down the other side"* AUTOCAR MAGAZINE, 1965

Not a very good car nor a particularly effective boat, the Amphicar nonetheless brought the concept of an amphibious automobile to the public.

Chrysler's extravagant showcase for its latest generation gas turbine engine, which in 1960 had already been tested on the road in a Dodge truck.

# CHRYSLER TURBOFLITE

By 1963, Chrysler was on track to do what no other carmaker had ever attempted—to make a gas-turbine-engined car and put it into the hands of consumers.

It first installed a gas-turbine engine into a Plymouth in 1954, and two years later felt confident enough to try a "real life" voyage from New York to Los Angeles, driven by Chrysler's research chief George Huebner. Some 50 further prototypes, and engines for laboratory-testing, were built until company bosses sanctioned the Turboflite.

The Chrysler Turboflite was presented as a showcase for the final CR2A engine—a unit said to weigh half as much as a conventional Chrysler V8, with only 60 moving parts instead of 300. It had been extensively road-tested in a Dodge truck in 1960.

The Turboflite's super-aggressive styling was by Chrysler's Maury Baldwin, with an enormous airfoil at the back sporting a pivoting lateral blade that was supposed to act as an airbrake to slow the car down. When either of the two doors were opened, the cockpit canopy automatically raised, using a pair of struts, to admit driver and passengers. A touch of the hot-rod was provided by the exposed front wheels and chrome frontal treatment. Luxuriously plump seating and electro-luminescent mood lighting created an inviting aura.

The Turboflite—which probably never ran under its own power—was built to Chrysler's precise design in Italy by revered coachbuilder Ghia, as a prelude to its manufacture of the Chrysler Turbine bodies.

## SPECIFICATION

**YEAR REVEALED** 1961

**PLACE OF ORIGIN** Detroit, Michigan, and Turin, Italy

**HISTORICAL STATUS** prototype

**ENGINE** gas turbine

**MAXIMUM POWER** 140bhp

**LAYOUT** front-mounted engine driving the rear wheels

**BODYWORK** two-door/single-canopy, four-seater coupé

**TOP SPEED** unknown

**NUMBER BUILT** one

*"Entrance-wise, the whole cockpit above the beltline lifted to admit passengers. The headlights were retractable. It was probably one of the best engineered show cars we ever did."*

MAURY BALDWIN, TURBOFLITE STYLIST

Showmanship overruled practicality for the Turboflite's lifting canopy.

Everyone knew that the Gyron would never appear in a Ford showroom; gyroscope-generated stability was an amusing idea, though.

# FORD GYRON

Automotive writers are often obliged to report guilelessly on concept cars, relaying the manufacturer's future visions at face value and seeking to maintain the industry's credibility. For once in 1961, though, Ford was not asking the world to believe it would be marketing a two-seater, two-wheeler gyroscope car any time soon. In fact, the US heavyweight was explicit: the Gyron was for show purposes only, where cunning anchoring on its display stand would ensure it stood upright in all its cartoonish glory.

Nonetheless, Ford couldn't put its pomposity entirely to one side. It insisted this self-balancing, aerodynamic, covered motorcycle just might be the sort of car we'd be driving in the 21st century.

The Gyron was the most ridiculous of a string of concepts to sally forth from Ford's Advanced Styling Studio, the product of Alex Tremulis. His other wacky creations included the six-wheeled Seattle-ite XXI and the sleek lines of the Ford Mexico coupé, as well as work on the Chrysler Thunderbolt and the Tucker Torpedo.

While the Gyron did not work, empty of both engine and gyroscopes, the public was asked to believe it would also incorporate computer-controlled navigation and cruise control functions. It was also supposed to have pop-out legs either side to support it at traffic lights.

Boys of the time must have absolutely loved the Gyron; perhaps their dads simply suppressed a wry chuckle.

## SPECIFICATION

**YEAR REVEALED** 1961

**PLACE OF ORIGIN** Detroit, Michigan

**HISTORICAL STATUS** prototype

**ENGINE** none fitted

**MAXIMUM POWER** unknown

**LAYOUT** not stated

**BODYWORK** single-canopy, two-seater coupé

**TOP SPEED** unknown

**NUMBER BUILT** one

*"At Ford in the 1950s and 1960s, dream cars went from just about credible to totally extreme. The Ford Gyron, which incorporated a huge gyroscope, was pure space-age imagination run wild."*

STEPHEN NEWBURY, *THE CAR DESIGN YEARBOOK 2*, 2003

# JAGUAR E-TYPE

The Jaguar E-type was derived from a racing car, and designed by an aerodynamics expert, not a "stylist." Its stiff chassis and independent suspension gave a smooth ride and brilliant roadholding. It also became a symbol of 1960s freedom.

At the 1961 Geneva Motor Show, the E-type emerged from a large wooden packing case as flashbulbs bounced off its aggressive, dart-like profile. Jaguar's streamlining guru Malcolm Sayer had adapted the sleek contours of the D-type racer into a pure road car, adding necessities such as bumpers, a proper hood, and even a practical hatchback third door on the coupé.

Demonstration cars loaned to magazines offered blistering performance from the 231ci (3,781cc) straight-six motor, with 149mph (240kph) attained for the roadster and the magic 150mph (241kph) for the coupé. But the cars are widely known now to have been "doctored"; a 140mph (225kph) maximum speed was nearer reality.

A bigger 258ci (4,235cc) engine from 1964 had more torque, an improved gearbox, better brakes, and comfier seats. Collectors highly rate this Series 1 4.2 E-type. The 1968 Series II was spoiled when its sleek headlight covers were dropped, and US pollution and safety laws necessitated less power and bigger bumpers. The E-type received a late-life image boost in 1971 when Jaguar used the car as a showcase for its V12 engine.

## SPECIFICATION

**YEAR REVEALED** 1961

**PLACE OF ORIGIN** Coventry, Warwickshire, UK

**HISTORICAL STATUS** production car

**ENGINE** six-cylinder, 231–258ci (3,781–4,235cc)

**MAXIMUM POWER** 246bhp

**LAYOUT** front-mounted engine driving the rear wheels

**BODYWORK** two-seater coupé and roadster and two-plus-two coupé

**TOP SPEED** 150mph (241kph)

**NUMBER BUILT** 72,007

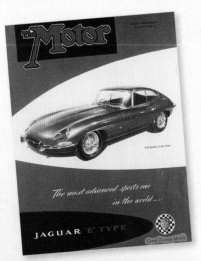

*"I want that car and I want it now."*

FRANK SINATRA, ON SEEING THE E-TYPE AT THE NEW YORK AUTO SHOW, APRIL 1961

Magazine covers were still sold as advertising space in 1961; the E-type was headline news anyhow.

The E-type remains one of the most desirable and evocative cars in motoring history; this is a Series II roadster.

Looking chic in Paris traffic, this example of the Renault 4 is in deluxe Parisienne trim, with fake wickerwork panels and gleaming wheel discs.

# RENAULT 4

As Renault's response to the utilitarian Citroën 2CV, the 4 was a long time coming, making its debut 13 years after the minimalist Citroën first delivered motoring to millions of French drivers. But for Renault, the car entered totally new territory on several fronts.

It was the company's first front-wheel drive car, although its engine was mounted longitudinally rather than transversely like the Mini's. It also pioneered the concept of a compact five-door hatchback with folding rear seats. It had several smaller innovations, such as a slightly different wheelbase on each side to facilitate a simple, cheap torsion bar rear suspension as part of the all-independent set-up. This meant the car had tight roadholding despite its propensity to lean alarmingly in any corner taken rapidly. A gearlever sprouting from the dashboard, offering gearchanges via a push/pull action, gave a flat, uncluttered floor.

The frugal and friendly 4 eventually became the biggest-selling French car ever. But it was a basic "tin can" to the end in 1993, which meant it stuck with features such as all-round sliding windows. The 68ci (1,108cc) engined GTL, of 1978, was more tolerable on long trips with higher gearing, bigger drum brakes, and cloth seats. Its gray plastic trimmings set it apart from the millions of older, more austere lookalikes rattling around Europe. Anyone wanting a more civilized 4 could always choose the Renault 6, built on an identical separate chassis platform.

---

## SPECIFICATION

**YEAR REVEALED**  1961

**PLACE OF ORIGIN**  Paris, France

**HISTORICAL STATUS**
production car

**ENGINE**  four-cylinder, 46–68ci (747–1,108cc)

**MAXIMUM POWER**  34bhp

**LAYOUT**  front-mounted engine driving the front wheels

**BODYWORK**  five-door, four-seater sedan

**TOP SPEED**  82mph (132kph)

**NUMBER BUILT**  8,135,422

---

*"Generous ground clearance is combined with soft, all-independent springing, which shows up magnificently upon the unmade, potholed roads sometimes found in new estates."*

ROAD TEST OF RENAULT 4L IN *MOTOR* MAGAZINE, 1962

Some early Renault 4s had the third side-window infilled to reduce the price.

Any driver of this Corvette Mako Shark show car might have yearned for the cooling ocean floor after sweltering under the clear plastic roof.

# CHEVROLET CORVETTE MAKO SHARK XP-755

It's one of the legendary stories of American car history—how, one day, head of General Motors Styling, William Mitchell, was out fishing off the Florida coast when he reeled in a short-fin mako shark. So smitten was he with this beautiful fish that he had it mounted on display in his office—its shimmering blue-to-white, graduated scales inspiring one of the most famous show cars General Motors ever produced.

The XP-755 was a glorious and arch two-seater roadster seemingly perfect for California living—a heady mixture of Italianate lines, racing car inspiration, and custom car detailing.

Outshining even the pointed prow and stern of the car, the snug cockpit with its panoramic windshield, transparent double-bubble hardtop with periscope rear mirror, and ostentatious exhaust pipes festooned along the body sides, the car's paintjob was breathtaking. A deep dark metallic blue on the top half of the body gradually faded to gleaming white, matching the oceanic shark's coloring.

Far from being a simple show exhibit, the XP-755, later christened Mako Shark I, was an important interim Corvette development. Clearly developing the theme of the 1961 Sting Ray Spider race/show car of 1961, the Mako Shark paved the way stylistically for the slightly toned-down 1963 Corvette Sting Ray cars, both designed for Mitchell by Larry Shinoda. The Mako Shark's supercharged engine was later swapped for a standard Chevrolet V8.

## SPECIFICATION

**YEAR REVEALED**  1962

**PLACE OF ORIGIN**  Detroit, Michigan

**HISTORICAL STATUS**  prototype

**ENGINE**  V8-cylinder, 328ci (5,360cc)

**MAXIMUM POWER**  456bhp

**LAYOUT**  front-mounted engine driving the rear wheels

**BODYWORK**  two-door, two-seater roadster

**TOP SPEED**  unknown

**NUMBER BUILT**  one

*"The iridescent blue top body fading to a white underbody was a real challenge for the paint technology of the day, but, when you look back, it was really a show-stopper."*

LARRY SHINODA, DESIGNER OF THE MAKO SHARK I

# FORD MUSTANG I

The Ford Mustang might have become another esoteric oddball in the footnotes of motoring history, but for the intervention of brash Italian-American Ford product planner Lee Iacocca. When Iacocca first saw this prototype in 1962, his instinctive grasp of America's unfolding demographics cut in immediately. The market craved a sporty car, not an actual sports car like this.

It featured a German Ford V4 engine mounted behind the driver and passenger, driving the rear wheels. In fact, it was the entire front-wheel drive, four-speed powerpack of the Ford Taunus 12M transferred to the back and cooled by radiators on each side, fed by two large air intakes. Suspension was by wishbones and coil springs, and there were front disc brakes.

The compact, dagger-shaped body featured an integrated rollover bar and retractable headlights. The seats were fixed as part of the structure, with steering wheel and pedals adjustable to suit any driver. The aluminum-skinned car was built by race-car preparers Troutman & Barnes, and named after the eponymous P-51 fighter plane.

Seeking credibility among enthusiasts, the Mustang made its public debut at the Watkins Glen race meeting in October 1962; top drivers Dan Gurney and Stirling Moss demonstrated it with bravura. However, by 1963, a Mustang II concept had taken shape, adapted from the conventional Ford Falcon. Here was the true predecessor to the "real" Mustang of 1964—the hottest thing to hit mainstream US motoring in a generation.

## SPECIFICATION

**YEAR REVEALED** 1962

**PLACE OF ORIGIN** Detroit, Michigan, and Culver City, California

**HISTORICAL STATUS** prototype

**ENGINE** V4-cylinder, 91ci (1,498cc)

**MAXIMUM POWER** 109bhp

**LAYOUT** mid-mounted engine driving the rear wheels

**BODYWORK** two-door, two-seater roadster

**TOP SPEED** 115mph (185kph)

**NUMBER BUILT** two

*"When I looked at the guys praising it, the offbeat crowd, the real buffs, I thought: 'That's sure not the car we want to build because it can't be a volume car. It's too far out.'"*

LEE IACOCCA, "FATHER" OF THE MUSTANG, IN *IACOCCA: AN AUTOBIOGRAPHY*, 1984

The Mustang that never was: only the name and copies of those distinctive air vents survived the transition to the "real thing" in 1964.

# SHELBY/AC COBRA

The Cobra was "invented" by Carroll Shelby, a Texas farmer and racing fanatic, who aimed to concoct a sports-racing car that could stand up to Ferrari.

His method was to shoehorn a muscular Ford Fairlane V8 260ci (4,261cc) engine into the "hull" of AC's Ace sports car. The simple, ladder-frame chassis and aluminum body were handbuilt in the UK by AC, and shipped unfinished to Shelby's auto workshops in California where the engines from Ford were fitted.

A sensation on the road, the Cobra was also born to race: the first British finisher at Le Mans in 1963, and scoring numerous victories in American events.

Ford later offered Shelby its bigger 289ci (4,736cc) engine but this was merely a stepping stone to the ultimate Cobra: the 427 of 1965. Conceived as a giant-killing race-winner, it boasted a big-block Ford Galaxie 500 V8. The 271bhp Cobra 289 was a performance legend, so this 427ci 425bhp (6,997cc) Cobra was phenomenal.

But despite a redesigned chassis and curved bodywork to accommodate fatter tires, the 427 had a short career: by 1965 it would have clashed with Ford's own GT40. Then safety and environmental legislation killed the Cobra in 1968. Today, originals are highly prized. An "official" AC MkIV has been available since 1983.

AC badge

## SPECIFICATION

**YEAR REVEALED** 1962

**PLACE OF ORIGIN** Thames Ditton, Surrey, UK, and Venice, California

**HISTORICAL STATUS** production car

**ENGINE** V8-cylinder, 260–427ci (4,261–6,997cc)

**MAXIMUM POWER** 425bhp

**LAYOUT** front-mounted engine driving the rear wheels

**BODYWORK** two-door, two-seater roadster

**TOP SPEED** 165mph (266kph)

**NUMBER BUILT** 979

*"Stabbing the throttle at rest produces a crisp, staccato crackle, with the characteristic V8 beat and a violent surge in revs. The same procedure with first engaged, and the clutch home, sends the car rocketing forward like a missile from a steam catapult."*

ROAD TEST OF AC COBRA 289, *AUTOCAR* MAGAZINE, 1965

The Cobra was the acme of pure, high-performance sports cars; there were several versions and this one is the UK-market AC 289.

Don't be surprised if you can detect aspects of subsequent cars in this profile of the Studebaker Avanti; the Loewy design proved highly influential.

# STUDEBAKER AVANTI

Conceived as an image-booster for the ailing Studebaker company, the fiberglass Avanti was a striking GT car. Studebaker president Sherwood Egbert first conceived such a sporting flagship but it was styled by Raymond Loewy, the legendary American industrial design genius most closely identified with the curvaceous Coca-Cola bottle.

The Avanti's unadorned and rakish lines were in sharp contrast to Detroit's normal, overblown, chrome-plated excess. The interior was modeled on a typical Italian sports car, with clear instruments and leather-clad bucket seats.

Showered with acclaim, the Avanti was destined for a short life luring buyers into Studebaker showrooms, because the company's bankrupt US car division shut down in 1964. While some production transferred to Canada, the Avanti was axed.

However, local Studebaker dealers Nate Altman and Leo Newman bought the rights to the car and vowed to continue making it. The Studebaker engine was obsolete, so they bought in Chevrolet Corvette units. Each Avanti II was now painstakingly hand-built.

The Avanti Motor Corporation became an institution, and survived profitably until 1982, when the families of Altman and Newman—both now dead—sold up. Subsequently, several entrepreneurs have hatched grand plans, revealed new models, and eventually transferred the car's production south to Mexico where, in theory, new Avantis are still available.

## SPECIFICATION

**YEAR REVEALED** 1962

**PLACE OF ORIGIN** South Bend, Indiana

**HISTORICAL STATUS** production car

**ENGINE** V8-cylinder, 289ci (4,736cc)

**MAXIMUM POWER** 335bhp

**LAYOUT** front-mounted engine driving the rear wheels

**BODYWORK** two-door four-seater coupé

**TOP SPEED** 145mph (233kph)

**NUMBER BUILT** 4,643

*"Both Egbert and Loewy had pretty definite ideas about what the car should be. Their ideas boil down to 14 mutually agreed upon requirements, the foremost of which were the disc brakes, built-in rollover bar, no useless ornamentation, no grille work, and no straight lines on the body."*

ROAD AND TRACK MAGAZINE, 1962

This Jeep Wagoneer Limited is a 1979 edition: its lines and tremendous off-road capability would survive for 12 further years.

# WILLYS JEEP WAGONEER

In the Wagoneer, the Sport Utility Vehicle (SUV) was crystalized. It was the first off-road vehicle with selectable four-wheel drive, purpose-designed to be just as suitable for cruising on highways.

The Wagoneer featured four doors. Its lofty bulk was cleverly masked by consultant designer Brooks Stevens, using visual tricks such as a waistline just below the side windows, slim window pillars, and suggestions of fenders and running boards pressed into the lower side panels.

The high-riding car also included a brand-new straight-six engine—the only American overhead-camshaft unit at the time. Here was a vehicle developed from the ground up, rather than being ultimately derived from the venerable war-time hero.

The legendary Jeep go-anywhere ability and image had been skillfully folded into the classic US station wagon to appeal to the latent weekender in most Americans, without sacrificing creature comforts. The Wagoneer, for instance, was the first off-roader with automatic transmission, and a choice of front suspensions: an independent set-up for leisure buyers most likely to be towing a trailer, or a solid front axle for heavy-duty off-roading.

It was the world's first purpose-designed SUV and also became the longest-lived. Just six months after the Wagoneer was unveiled, the "Willys" name was ditched and Jeep became a marque in its own right. Despite frequent cosmetic makeovers, the Wagoneer remained a timeless icon until 1992.

## SPECIFICATION

**YEAR REVEALED** 1962

**PLACE OF ORIGIN** Toledo, Ohio

**HISTORICAL STATUS** production car

**ENGINE** six-cylinder, 230ci (3,769cc), V8-cylinder, 349ci (5,724cc)

**MAXIMUM POWER** 230bhp

**LAYOUT** front-mounted engine driving all four wheels

**BODYWORK** four-door, five-seater station wagon

**TOP SPEED** 85mph (137kph)

**NUMBER BUILT** unknown

*"These added horses let the Wagoneer cruise quietly at 75mph, give it bags of low-speed torque, and enable it to crawl up any hill it can get traction on."*

ROAD TEST OF WAGONEER WITH V8 ENGINE BY BOB MCVAY, *MOTOR TREND* MAGAZINE, 1965

The 1963 Hillman Imp was an unusual small machine by any measure, with its rear-mounted, all-aluminum engine and opening rear window through which light luggage could be accessed. It was an appealing car but one beset by problems, some of which were caused by the fact that politicians insisted it be built near Glasgow, Scotland, hundreds of miles from Hillman's Coventry base; engines were transported up there by train, and finished cars—as here—headed south again on open rail cars.

The impact of the Testudo may be lost today compared to subsequent designs, but Giugiaro's smooth styling was, for the time, ground-breaking.

# BERTONE TESTUDO

The Testudo may look as extreme as any "dream" car of the early 1960s, but it had one crucial difference: it worked.

Almost as impressive is the fact that the Testudo was conceived and constructed in a mere two months, from January to March 1963, causing a wave of excitment when exhibited at the Geneva Motor Show.

Smooth and aerodynamic, the car's windshield, glass roof, and doors all hinged forward as a giant, one-piece canopy to admit driver and passenger. The lack of windshield pillars was matched by a thin instrument panel set into the dashboard, where the main feature was a prominent grab handle for the passenger—after all, the driver had the steering wheel to hold on to while hauling himself over the high sill.

The very low frontal area, with no radiator grille and headlights that swiveled up from their lie-flat position on the hood when switched on, was made possible because the car used the floorpan of the rear-engined Chevrolet Corvair Monza. Air was drawn to the flat-six engine in the tail through intakes just aft of the canopy.

On a hot day, with the sun blazing down through the glass top, the Testudo would no doubt have been unbearable. But in spring 1963, conditions were almost perfect for driving the Testudo, which Nuccio Bertone did from his Turin headquarters to the Geneva Motor Show; this was a long trip across the Alps, making the journey even more of an achievement for such a hastily completed concept car.

## SPECIFICATION

**YEAR REVEALED** 1963

**PLACE OF ORIGIN** Turin, Italy

**HISTORICAL STATUS** prototype

**ENGINE** flat-six-cylinder, 164ci (2,683cc)

**MAXIMUM POWER** 142bhp

**LAYOUT** rear-mounted engine driving the rear wheels

**BODYWORK** single-canopy, two-seater coupé

**TOP SPEED** unknown

**NUMBER BUILT** one

*"Then [in 1963], the St Bernardo and Mont Blanc tunnels linking Italy with Switzerland did not exist. It was undoubtedly a demonstration of faith in the reliability of the Testudo."*

BERTONE PRESS RELEASE, 1995

The lift-up canopy is demonstrated here, along with different wheels.

# ASTON MARTIN DB5

For some moviegoers, the real star of *Goldfinger*, James Bond's third big movie adventure, wasn't Sean Connery but a silver Aston Martin DB5.

Bond's most impressive on-screen gadget, the Aston all but stole the show when Bond's captor was sent hurtling through the roof in an ejector seat. Replicas of the "Goldfinger" DB5 toured the world, drawing huge crowds years after the 1964 film had left theaters.

The fifth Aston wasn't a new car but a refinement of the 226ci (3,700cc) DB4 first seen in 1958. Handcrafted in aluminum over a tubular steel frame, with a bigger, 244ci (3,995cc) version of the twin-camshaft six-cylinder engine—offering 240bhp— and a five-speed ZF gearbox, Aston Martin claimed more punch with longer legs.

Top speed was 140mph (225kph)—nearer 150mph (241kph) from the tuned "Vantage" engine—with meaty acceleration to match.

The DB5 kept pace with technical developments, rather than breaking new ground. Disc brakes were fitted all round but independent rear suspension was eschewed for a traditional solid back axle: hence the DB5 was happier on fast main roads than being hurried through tight corners.

Faired-in headlights updated the aerodynamics and the inside featured rich leather upholstery, electric windows, and a push-button radio.

As well as the fastback, Aston built the swish Volante convertible, and even 12 "shooting brake" DB5s. The DB5 is one of the most memorable Aston Martins ever.

## SPECIFICATION

**YEAR REVEALED** 1963

**PLACE OF ORIGIN** Newport Pagnell, Buckinghamshire, UK

**HISTORICAL STATUS** production car

**ENGINE** six-cylinder, 244ci (3,995cc)

**MAXIMUM POWER** 314bhp

**LAYOUT** front-mounted engine driving the rear wheels

**BODYWORK** two-door four-seater coupé and convertible

**TOP SPEED** 150mph (241kph)

**NUMBER BUILT** 1,063

*"It is a car requiring skill and muscle—a man's car—which challenges and satisfies and always excites."* ROAD TEST, *AUTOCAR* MAGAZINE, 1964

The gorgeous side profile of the DB5 was a refinement of Touring's original DB4.

Sean Connery poses with the Aston Martin DB5, made almost as famous as 007 by its appearance in *Goldfinger*, released in 1964.

# CHRYSLER TURBINE

Chrysler's Turbine project was the most glamorous rolling experiment ever conducted on American roads. The only car ever series-produced with a gas-turbine "jet" engine, the real-life test program went as smoothly as the power delivery from its vibration-free power unit.

Selling the car to the public was deemed too risky, so Chrysler loaned examples for free, for three-month trial periods, to a wide spectrum of American drivers. Rather than install the fourth-generation engine in a standard Chrysler, a unique model was designed in-house. The bodies were built by Italian coachbuilder Ghia and power units fitted in Detroit. The Turbine was a four-seater hardtop with little of the jet-age gimmickry of most Chrysler/Ghia show cars.

The speed of the engine was reduced to a maximum of 4,680rpm in daily driving use and the power was delivered to the wheels via a lightly modified automatic gearbox. The engine could burn any fuel, including diesel, kerosene, alcohol, or vegetable fat.

The test cars proved remarkably reliable, with only 5 percent of the total test time lost to breakdowns, and oil changes unnecessary. Downsides included patchy running at high altitudes and the vacuum cleaner-like noise. But the biggest problem was the unacceptably high level of nitrogen oxide emissions. After the program ended in September 1966, 46 Turbines were scrapped; today, three working cars survive. Chrysler's financial troubles meant the Turbine adventure was never repeated.

## SPECIFICATION

**YEAR REVEALED** 1963

**PLACE OF ORIGIN** Detroit, Michigan, and Turin, Italy

**HISTORICAL STATUS** production car

**ENGINE** gas turbine

**MAXIMUM POWER** 130bhp

**LAYOUT** front-mounted engine driving the rear wheels

**BODYWORK** two-door, four-seater hardtop coupé

**TOP SPEED** unknown

**NUMBER BUILT** 55

*"With no carburetor, you don't pump the throttle as you would for other cars of the era. Acceleration is progressive and oh-so-smooth, but it's not terribly quick. Drivers will marvel at the sound rather than the forward thrust."* TODD LASSA, *MOTOR TREND* MAGAZINE, 2007

In this period image, two of the 55 Chrysler Turbines built show their salient features, although the real whirr of excitement was under the hood.

# EXCALIBUR SS

The US's *Time* magazine called Brooks Stevens "The seer who made Milwaukee famous." In 61 years of industrial design, he had 550 clients and created thousands of pieces of work, including several cars. In 1950, he single-handedly created the "recreational" off-road market with his design for the Jeep Jeepster, a sort of four-wheel drive sports car.

His eclectic Excalibur J sports-racing car appeared in 1952, but in 1963, he hit the nascent nostalgia movement with the Excalibur SS show car, featuring a Studebaker Lark chassis and supercharged V8 engine.

It was the star attraction at the 1963 New York Auto Show, and Stevens was deluged with orders. He adapted the chassis to accept a Chevrolet Corvette engine, setting it back over 2ft (60cm) in the frame for authentic vintage proportions. Flexible metal exhaust pipes were proudly carried along the sides, the radiator shell was aluminum, and the body panels were fiberglass.

Stevens's two sons then offered the Excalibur SS to the public, adding Roadster and four-seater Phaeton editions. Although scorned by vintage enthusiasts, they were a hit with drivers who craved the attention of passers-by.

## SPECIFICATION

**YEAR REVEALED** 1963

**PLACE OF ORIGIN** Milwaukee, Wisconsin

**HISTORICAL STATUS** production car

**ENGINE** V8-cylinder, 327ci (5,362cc)

**MAXIMUM POWER** 300bhp

**LAYOUT** front-mounted engine driving the rear wheels

**BODYWORK** door-less and then two-door, two-seater roadster and four-seater convertible

**TOP SPEED** 140mph (225kph)

**NUMBER BUILT** 359

*"It is not an accurately scaled-down replica, but more in the nature of a modern version, designed to have the 'feel' of the original."*

ROAD TEST OF SS PROTOTYPE, *ROAD & TRACK* MAGAZINE, 1964

It didn't matter that the car wasn't a faithful Mercedes replica—the Excalibur SS still oozed nostalgia.

# NSU WANKEL SPIDER

A rotary engine is any power unit that dispenses with a crankshaft to eliminate reciprocal motion, giving near-perfect balance. German engineer Dr. Felix Wankel perfected the technology for road transport and, in 1964, the first car of its kind went on sale thanks to NSU, a German maker of scooters and economy cars.

Wankel's rotary engine had a single, shallow, lozenge-shaped combustion chamber in which a near-triangular rotary "piston" spun eccentrically.

Wankel first envisaged rotary engines in 1924, and NSU became interested in his research and patents to boost performance of its racing motorcycles. Prototype engines were running by 1958 and the partners worked closely to resolve design issues.

By putting the engine into small-scale production in a specialized sports car, its reliability could be assessed without jeopardizing NSU's profitability.

The Spider hit the headlines in September 1963, and production starting the following year. The tiny Wankel engine was mounted under the trunk floor at the back: with a single rotor, the Spider could almost reach 100mph (161kph). What it lacked in torque it made up for in free-revving smoothness, spinning happily to 8,000rpm. Critics praised its power delivery and handling, but the Spider, like all early rotaries, needed plentiful fuel and maintenance. Dr. Wankel, though, never experienced the thrill of driving it on open roads—he never had a driver's license.

## SPECIFICATION

**YEAR REVEALED** 1963

**PLACE OF ORIGIN** Neckarsulm, West Germany

**HISTORICAL STATUS** production car

**ENGINE** single-rotor rotary, 30ci (497cc)

**MAXIMUM POWER** 50bhp

**LAYOUT** rear-mounted engine driving the rear wheels

**BODYWORK** two-door, two-seater roadster

**TOP SPEED** 97mph (156kph)

**NUMBER BUILT** 2,375

This ghosted illustration shows just how compact the engine was.

*"The odd thing about the Wankel is that it gets progressively smoother as its speed builds up, with no vibration periods, valve bounce, or the like to impose limits on it."*

ROAD TEST OF THE SPIDER IN *ROAD & TRACK* MAGAZINE, 1965

With styling from Bertone, the Spider was an experiment in building rotary-engined production cars, with problems ironed out as they arose.

One of the first 911s: it acted as a springboard for future success, with performance escalating constantly.

# PORSCHE 911

Dr Ferdinand Porsche and his son, also Ferdinand (Ferry), found enormous success with the first Porsche, the 356. However, as the 1960s dawned, Porsche's links to Volkswagen were creating limitations. The next Porsche phase started in 1963 when the 911 was unveiled. When the car reached lucky customers in 1964 (the 911 was always expensive), they found a radical evolution of the 356. The stylish lines were an admirable attempt, by Ferry's own industrial designer son Butzi Porsche, to keep the car as pure and as functional as possible. And an entirely new flat-six engine lay under the sloping tail. It was still air-cooled, in the Beetle tradition,

Porsche badge

and its 73ci (1,991cc) offered 130bhp. But the engine had enormous potential for increasing the power. This was the key reason the 911 remained in production, fundamentally unchanged, until 1996. In its ultimate, twin-turbocharged, four-wheel-drive form, it produced 408bhp.

Back in 1963, Porsche showed off the car's clever steering system which, because it ran along the floor, enabled a low frontal area, decent front luggage space, and easy collapsibility in a crash.

Tail-happy handling due to the weight bias is part of the 911's mystique; devotees relish the driving challenge that comes with sitting behind the wheel of a 911.

## SPECIFICATION

**YEAR REVEALED** 1963

**PLACE OF ORIGIN** Stuttgart, West Germany

**HISTORICAL STATUS** production car

**ENGINE** flat-six-cylinder, 73–220ci (1,991–3,600cc)

**MAXIMUM POWER** 408bhp

**LAYOUT** rear-mounted engine driving the rear or all four wheels

**BODYWORK** four-seater coupé, Targa-convertible and convertible

**TOP SPEED** 180mph (290kph)

**NUMBER BUILT** 456,047

*"In side winds, the 911 remains stable, a quality difficult to obtain on any car with a low-drag body, and particularly so when the engine is located at the rear."*

ROAD TEST, *MOTOR TREND* MAGAZINE, 1965

# FORD GT40

In 1962, Henry Ford II began negotiations to buy Ferrari, in order to sprinkle some much-needed racing stardust on the increasingly dull company his grandfather had founded in 1903. Victory in the Le Mans 24-hour race was the main aim.

Why Enzo Ferrari recoiled at the eleventh hour is still unclear, but Ford decided to beat Ferrari at his own game. Coincidentally, British racing car constructor Lola had just completed a mid-engined Mk6 GT car using a Ford V8 engine that showed enormous promise. An opportune Ford bought the project and engaged Lola founder Eric Broadley to develop it.

Ford's involvement was often detrimental. It handled the styling, which wasn't aerodynamic enough at race speeds. It also wanted the "GT40" to be factory-made, insisting on a cheap steel monocoque rather than Broadley's aluminum "tub," making it unnecessarily heavy.

At Le Mans in 1965, Ferrari won. A re-designed GT40 then won Le Mans four times between 1966 and 1969. The first victory in the hands of New Zealanders Bruce McLaren and Chris Amon also saw the GT40 become the first car to cover 3,000 miles (4,828km) in the race.

By 1967, Ford withdrew from racing, but a private team took two other Le Mans wins with the GT40. In 1969, Jacky Ickx beat Hans Herrmann's Porsche by 328ft (100 meters)—the closest to a photo-finish the race has seen. The MkIII was solely for road use, but of the 107 built, just 31 were road cars.

## SPECIFICATION

**YEAR REVEALED** 1964

**PLACE OF ORIGIN** Slough, Berkshire, UK

**HISTORICAL STATUS** sports-racer/ production car

**ENGINE** V8-cylinder, 288ci (4,727cc)

**MAXIMUM POWER** 335bhp (MkIII road car), 485bhp+ in race tune

**LAYOUT** mid-mounted engine driving the rear wheels

**BODYWORK** two-seater coupé

**TOP SPEED** 200mph+ (322kph+)

**NUMBER BUILT** 107

*"I supervised the design of the chassis. I was, and am, a purist and the brief changed. But the GT40 was, in the end, a very sophisticated design that did a good job. Ford did have luck on its side, though: Ferrari was weak at the time."*

ERIC BROADLEY, FOUNDER OF LOLA AND GT40 DEVELOPMENT ENGINEER, 2003

Ford masterminded the GT40 after having its takeover of Ferrari rebuffed; this one is being driven by Peter Sutcliffe in the 1966 Spa 500km race.

This attempt at the World land speed record failed when the Proteus-Bluebird CN7 crashed. The rebuilt car, though, returned to Utah in 1964 and achieved 403.10mph (648.7kph).

# AUSTIN/FLM PANELCRAFT TAXI

Nubar Sarkis Gulbenkian, monocle in right eye and orchid always on lapel, was one of London's most recognizable playboys during the 1960s. He lived at the Ritz Hotel, married three times, and enjoyed a lifestyle of supreme indulgence.

He was of Armenian-Jewish extraction and, like his father Calouste Gulbenkian, made his fortune in the Middle East oil industry. Old Calouste's acumen at deal-making meant he eventually owned 5 percent of the shares in oil company BP. Nubar was no less astute, but enjoyed more of his fortune than his father ever had.

Motoring was a Gulbenkian passion. At first, it was ultra-fast vintage sports cars; then a string of specially made, and mostly very ugly, Rolls-Royces.

In 1965, Nubar decided to have a unique miniature limousine built—based on London's superbly maneuverable Austin FX4 taxi. A bewildered Rolls-Royce was asked to assist, and construction was eventually entrusted to the workshops of FLM Panelcraft in London's Battersea. Soon, a rear passenger compartment resembling a horse-drawn Brougham was built on to the cab's familiar frontage. The interior featured gold-plated fittings, there were carriage lamps on the door pillars, and the hood sported a Lalique glass mascot.

It instantly became one of London's most distinctive cars, and Gulbenkian ordered a second example. The first taxi went to California. It still exists, however, making £23,000 at a British auction in the 1990s.

## SPECIFICATION

**YEAR REVEALED** 1965

**PLACE OF ORIGIN** Coventry, Warwickshire, and London, UK

**HISTORICAL STATUS** customized production car

**ENGINE** four-cylinder, 129ci (2,199cc)

**MAXIMUM POWER** 68bhp

**LAYOUT** front-mounted engine driving the rear wheels

**BODYWORK** four-door, six-seater sedan

**TOP SPEED** 80mph (129kph)

**NUMBER BUILT** two

*"I like to travel in a gold-plated taxi that can turn on a sixpence—whatever that is."*

NUBAR GULBENKIAN

Throughout the late 1960s, this bizarre modified taxi—containing tycoon playboy Nubar Gulbenkian—was a regular sight in high-society London.

# GOLDENROD

Goldenrod—still the world's fastest conventional "car"—was built by Californian brothers Bill and Bob Summers who dreamed of an assault on the World land speed record.

Bob built a scale model and mapped out its layout to demonstrate how his car could become the fastest vehicle on earth. Chrysler was so impressed it agreed to provide the engines, and Goldenrod was born.

Goldenrod was essentially a four-wheel drive, 32ft- (10m-) long javelin. The four fuel-injected Chrysler V8 engines were set in pairs in the chassis, mounted back-to-back. The front pair drove the front wheels and rear pair the rear ones, with a mechanical coupling to synchronize the 2,400bhp power output.

Bob Summers calculated that Goldenrod's weight would keep its aluminum wheels and Firestone tires glued to the white surface of Bonneville Salt Flats, Utah. Goldenrod took the record for a wheel-driven car from Britain's Donald Campbell, returning it to the US for the first time since 1928. In 1991, Al Teague's "Spirit of 76" slightly bettered the speed for a piston-engined car, but that was supercharged.

## SPECIFICATION

**YEAR REVEALED**  1965

**PLACE OF ORIGIN**  Ontario, California

**HISTORICAL STATUS**  speed record car

**ENGINE**  four x V8-cylinder, 421ci (6,900cc)

**MAXIMUM POWER**  2,400bhp

**LAYOUT**  four engines mounted in a row, driving all four wheels

**BODYWORK**  single-canopy, single-seater racer

**TOP SPEED**  409mph (658kph)

**NUMBER BUILT**  one

*"It means so much to the world of hot-rodding. For nearly 40 years, the Goldenrod has held one of the most significant records on anyone's books."*

HOT ROD MAGAZINE, 2008

Bob Summers stands by Goldenrod at the Bonneville Salt Flats in 1965.

# OLDSMOBILE TORONADO

Introduced to the public on October 14, 1965, the luxurious Toronado was America's first front-wheel drive car since the Cord 810, 30 years earlier. Its clean styling was a landmark—rated by William Mitchell, studio chief at the time, as one of the best-looking General Motors cars ever.

Heavily flared wheelarches suggested enormous wheels, its rear wings and roof pillars blended into one smooth plane, and retractable headlamps added to frontal elegance. Oldsmobile's engineers deemed the shape perfect for the front-wheel drive platform they'd spent seven years perfecting.

Front-drive "XP-784" prototypes disguised with Oldsmobile 98 bodies had undergone an unprecedented 1.5 million miles (2.4 million kilometers) of road testing.

Consequently, the Toronado was over-engineered, with beefed-up Hydramatic automatic transmission and even custom Firestone tires with stiffened sidewalls.

Torsion bar front suspension was chosen for its compactness, and at the back was a beam axle on leaf springs. Suspension, powertrain, and floorpan were all carried in a large subframe, to limit noise and vibration transfer to the passengers. The sole weakness was its all-drum brakes, which were prone to fading; front discs remedied that.

This Oldsmobile drew acclaim for its traction and roadholding, receiving *Motor Trend* magazine's Car Of The Year award. The first-generation car lasted until 1970. The Toronado name, however, while dynamic-sounding, was totally meaningless.

## SPECIFICATION

**YEAR REVEALED** 1965

**PLACE OF ORIGIN** Detroit, Michigan

**HISTORICAL STATUS** production car

**ENGINE** V8-cylinder, 425–454ci (6,965–7,446cc)

**MAXIMUM POWER** 400bhp

**LAYOUT** front-mounted engine driving the front wheels

**BODYWORK** two-door, four-seater coupé

**TOP SPEED** 135mph (217kph)

**NUMBER BUILT** 143,134

*"The Toronado is like most American cars, with all the vices and virtues that entails—but with superior handling under adverse road conditions, and slightly better space utilization"*

ROAD TEST IN *ROAD & TRACK* MAGAZINE, 1965

Regarded as one of the most accomplished designs America produced in the 1960s, the Toronado was also an unlikely front-wheel drive pioneer.

This later Europa was much improved over earlier models for driver comfort, but it was hard to better the already exceptional roadholding.

# LOTUS EUROPA

It was 42in (106cm) tall and, at 0.29, its drag coefficient made it highly aerodynamic. Most people thought the Lotus Europa's compressed appearance was madcap, but suspected there must be a good scientific reason. They were right. It was the first proper production road car with a mid-mounted engine, bringing the Formula One configuration to the streets.

Lotus founder Colin Chapman found a perfect drivetrain in the Renault 16. Although a family hatchback, Chapman realised its 90ci (1,470cc) transverse engine, four-speed transmission, and front-wheel drive package was light and compact enough to install at the center of the Elan's backbone chassis, to achieve that authentic Formula One handling response.

Renault gladly supplied its components and the car was, appropriately, christened Lotus Europe, although quickly changed to Europa for trademark registration reasons.

There was only 78bhp on tap, so a top speed of just 95mph (153kph) wasn't surprising. The clutch was heavy, the ride poor. But the car gripped in corners like nothing else, with light steering and a feeling of perfect balance, partly down to rear suspension by lower wishbones and transverse top links.

Europa drivers enjoyed a sunlounger driving position, but the cockpit was claustrophobic because the side windows didn't open and rear vision was awful. Lotus tackled the car's appearance and design, reinvigorating Europa until 1975.

## SPECIFICATION

**YEAR REVEALED**  1966

**PLACE OF ORIGIN**  Hethel, Norfolk, UK

**HISTORICAL STATUS**  production car

**ENGINE**  four-cylinder, 90–97ci (1,470–1,588cc)

**MAXIMUM POWER**  126bhp

**LAYOUT**  mid-mounted engine driving the rear wheels

**BODYWORK**  two-door, two-seater coupé

**TOP SPEED**  121mph (195kph)

**NUMBER BUILT**  9,230

*"The Europa Twin Cam can still out-corner nearly anything on the road, and we could not fault the brakes on this car."*

ROAD TEST, *MOTOR* MAGAZINE, 1971

Nuccio Bertone inspects the Bertone Carabo, complete with scissor-doors that became a feature found on later Lamborghinis.

# BERTONE CARABO

The Carabo sits at the pinnacle of the "wedge" car design craze of the late 1960s and early 1970s. Along with a galaxy of other concept cars, this fantasy machine took groundhugging to extremes. Bertone used a mid-engined layout to turn what would normally have been a hood into an acute-angled nosecone, from which the enormous windshield was a continuation in one unbroken styling line. An abruptly truncated tail hinted at scientific aerodynamics, but the main intention of these cars was to shock and impress in equal measures.

There seems to be no evidence that the quoted 160mph (257kph) of the Carabo was ever attained, but its stunning lines— the work of designer Marcello Gandini—

certainly cloaked a real car. In this case, the chassis was from the Alfa Romeo Tipo 33 race car with a V8 engine, complete with its sophisticated all-round double-wishbone suspension and disc brakes.

Bertone's deft public relations made the Carabo a headline-grabber around the world upon its unveiling at the 1968 Paris Motor Show on its looks alone. Yet it was also a technology showcase, boasting lightweight copper-tinted glass from Belgian specialists VHR-Glabverbel, and a metallic green paint job with fluorescent orange highlights.

No one claimed the Carabo would be on sale any time soon, yet, three years later, this was clearly the inspiration for the Lamborghini Countach—adding to the car's iconic status in the pantheon of car design.

## SPECIFICATION

**YEAR REVEALED** 1968

**PLACE OF ORIGIN** Turin, Italy

**HISTORICAL STATUS** prototype

**ENGINE** V8-cylinder, 123ci (1,995cc)

**MAXIMUM POWER** 230bhp

**LAYOUT** mid-mounted engine driving the rear wheels

**BODYWORK** two-door, two-seater coupé

**TOP SPEED** 160mph (257kph) (claimed)

**NUMBER BUILT** one

*"A landmark, for many years nobody went beyond it. You could put it into a show now and it would still impress."*

*AUTOCAR MAGAZINE, 1977*

By the late 1960s, and driven by tireless campaigners like Ralph Nader, safety could no longer be ignored. This explains Volkswagen's employment of these willing crash test dummies.

# CHITTY CHITTY BANG BANG

Count Louis Zborowski was something of a showman. He built four colossal aeroplane-engined cars in the 1920s. They were as much as 1,648ci (27,000cc) in size, and widely known as "Chitty Chitty Bang Bangs"; rarely revving above 1,500rpm.

One man they left an indelible impression on was James Bond creator Ian Fleming, who wrote a 1964 children's book based on the story of a similarly large vintage car with magical powers. Three years later, Albert "Cubby" Broccoli, producer of the 007 movies, turned Fleming's fairytale into a film, with the help of author Roald Dahl, which was first screened in December 1968.

The cinematic Chitty Chitty Bang Bang was no aero-engined leviathan but was specially built by Alan Mann Racing. It had a V6 Ford 183ci (2,994cc) engine and automatic transmission, and was designed to withstand mistreatment during filming but to retain a hand-made coachbuilt aura. Production designer Ken Adam and special effects guru Rowland Whett made Chitty appear to fly and swim, as lovable inventor Caractacus Potts—played by Dick Van Dyke—intended.

Broccoli kept the car at Pinewood Studios but sold it to professional clown Pierre Picton in 1972, with a proviso that Broccoli had first refusal if he got sick of it. That was probably the reason Picton turned down an offer for the car from pop star Michael Jackson in 1991, reputedly for over $10 million.

## SPECIFICATION

**YEAR REVEALED** 1968

**PLACE OF ORIGIN** Weybridge, Surrey, UK

**HISTORICAL STATUS** custom-made movie car

**ENGINE** V6-cylinder, 183ci (2,994cc)

**MAXIMUM POWER** 136bhp

**LAYOUT** front-mounted engine driving the rear wheels

**BODYWORK** door-less, four-seater convertible

**TOP SPEED** unknown

**NUMBER BUILT** four (three of them mock-ups for filming)

*"Mr. Broccoli's men added wings and propellers to one and a hovercraft skirt to another. Mann found some extra grip by persuading Goodyear to mold the tires from their newest racing compound."*

*FORD TIMES* MAGAZINE, 1968

theater lobby card advertising the film *Chitty Chitty Bang Bang*.

You'd never guess there was a modern Ford V6 engine under that vintage-style hood, and nor that those "wooden" wheels were cast aluminum.

# IKENGA

The shimmering blue Ikenga made its public debut in London's Harrods department store in October 1968. It was the dreamchild of Brooklyn-born, 29-year-old David Gittens, and 30,000 people flocked to admire it.

Gittens' work as an advertising photographer brought him to London in 1964, and a casual chat one day about the tarnished image of British cars was the impetus to design his own. But he needed help to build it, a chassis, and hard cash.

The first came from race engineer Ken Sheppard and north London body-builders, Williams & Pritchard. The mid-engined chassis was from a secondhand Mclaren Mk1 racing car. And finally, Copleys merchant bank in the City provided the finance.

At 38in (97cm) high, it was extreme, with the entire front and rear sections of the car swinging open, clamshell-style, to reveal the cramped, leather-clad two-seater cockpit with square, tilt-away steering wheel, and Chevrolet Camaro Z28 engine. But when Charlie Williams, who built the body, died in 1969, plans to make the car with American backing fell apart. Gittens returned to the US, the only prototype seized by his main creditor, Copleys Bank.

## SPECIFICATION

**YEAR REVEALED** 1968

**PLACE OF ORIGIN** London, UK

**HISTORICAL STATUS** prototype

**ENGINE** V8-cylinder, 396ci (6,489cc)

**MAXIMUM POWER** 325bhp

**LAYOUT** mid-mounted engine driving the rear wheels

**BODYWORK** single-canopy, two-seater coupé

**TOP SPEED** 162mph (261kph) (claimed)

**NUMBER BUILT** one

*"I walked into some companies and said: 'I have a car and I think this will be an answer to the Lamborghini—and a very representative car of England'. Enough of them agreed to co-operate so we could get the whole thing going."*

INTERVIEW WITH DAVID GITTENS, *CAR AND DRIVER* MAGAZINE, 1969

It took an African-American photographer to shake up the sleepy British car industry and help him build the Ikenga.

# 5

## 1970–1979

# FUEL CRISIS AND MOON LANDINGS

From an automotive viewpoint, the 1970s was dominated by the fuel crisis that engulfed the first half of the decade, and the uncertain motoring outlook that ensued.

Although the early 1970s would see some iconic high-performance, wedge-shaped "supercars" come to life, large-engined mass-market cars suffered, out of favor for their fuel thirst and their harmful impact on the environment.

While alternative fuels, electricity in particular, were hot topics, the real progress was made in the Far East, where Japan's output of automobiles was thrifty, efficient, and affordable. They may have been scorned in Europe and the US to begin with, but Japanese cars were also well-made, forcing Western rivals to up their game or—as some discovered—face oblivion.

But it wasn't all doom and gloom. New model designs were increasingly attractive and well equipped while, on the world's race tracks, lateral thinking produced giant steps in aerodynamics. Engineers even developed a car that could be driven on the Moon.

# BOND BUG

Britain's most parochial maker of economy cars and an Austrian-born industrial designer put this adventurous car into mass production.

Reliant was Britain's biggest three-wheeled vehicle manufacturer when, in 1963, it contracted Ogle Design—a leading product consultancy—to improve its image. Coincidentally, Ogle's managing director Tom Karen had planned his own tiny three-wheeled fun car, called the Rascal, back in 1958. Aimed at students, it was designed to be cheap to make and own.

At first, Karen was occupied with Reliant's innovative Scimitar GTE sports-station wagon, but by 1967 his client was eager to add his sporty three-wheeler to its line-up. The final production car was amazingly faithful to Karen's proposal, including the vertically truncated tail, the exposed rear axle, and even a plywood trunk lid. Reliant insisted on more luggage space within the plastic body, but actually made the car more radical by incorporating a lift-up canopy with side-screens, instead of a fixed roof.

The car went on sale in June 1970 as the Bond Bug, the Bond marque having been acquired by Reliant that year. It could be bought with Reliant's "credit package" offering time purchase, a two-year warranty and cheap insurance, designed to foster sales among young drivers.

It was quite exhilarating to drive despite its meager power, yet the Bug was a small seller and was dropped in 1974, unable to overcome the Mini's four-wheeled allure.

## SPECIFICATION

**YEAR REVEALED** 1970

**PLACE OF ORIGIN** Preston, Lancashire, and Tamworth, Staffordshire, UK

**HISTORICAL STATUS** production car

**ENGINE** four-cylinder, 43–46ci (701–748cc)

**MAXIMUM POWER** 35bhp

**LAYOUT** front-mounted engine driving the rear wheels

**BODYWORK** single-canopy, two-seater sedan

**TOP SPEED** 77mph (124kph)

**NUMBER BUILT** 2,268

*"It's fast, safe, and above all fun. The sight of this little projectile beetling past more staid sedans produces many a startled look."* ROAD TEST, *MOTOR* MAGAZINE, 1970

Bond Bug sales literature was redolent of the bright, youthful hopes of the 1970s.

The Bond Bug's radical wedge shape, plus its three-wheeled configuration and single-canopy door, produced a different kind of economy car.

The Citroën SM had a wide front-wheel drive stance tapering inward to a narrower-track rear. Under its hood lay the wonder of Maserati power.

# CITROËN SM

Citroën had long plotted a genuine flagship model mixing the DS's high-tech logic with two extra facets: performance and prestige. Therefore, the opportunity to buy Italy's Maserati in 1968 proved ideal for adding supercar experience to Citroën's renowned design ideals.

The result, in 1970, was the fabulous Citroën SM, a stunning combination of French ingenuity and Italian panache. At its heart was a tidy 90 degree V6 Maserati engine, derived from the marque's V8. At 163ci (2,670cc), it put the car just inside the acceptable bracket for taxation in France.

Unlike a Maserati, however, the SM was front-wheel drive, with the transmission and driveshafts mounted ahead of the set-back engine. This superb weight distribution promoted stable road manners, but Citroën's hydro-pneumatic self-levelling suspension, plus four-wheel disc brakes, were excellent features, too. The headlamps could swivel with the self-centring, power steering, allowing an SM to "see around corners."

But the body design topped that. With a frontal glass fairing and aircraft-grade aluminum hood, the SM tapered to a sleek finish with a glass tailgate. The huge windshield and sheathed rear wheels had a space-age aura. The cabin brimmed with futuristic touches, such as oval dials and a single-spoke steering wheel. The seats, with broad, sculptural rolls, looked amazing despite being unsupportive. But sadly, the 1973 global fuel crisis meant demand for 18mpg (6.4km/l) cars evaporated overnight.

## SPECIFICATION

**YEAR REVEALED**  1970

**PLACE OF ORIGIN**  Paris, France, and Modena, Italy

**HISTORICAL STATUS**  production car

**ENGINE**  V6-cylinder, 163–181ci (2,670–2,974cc)

**MAXIMUM POWER**  180bhp

**LAYOUT**  front-mounted engine driving the front wheels

**BODYWORK**  two-door, four-seater sedan

**TOP SPEED**  142mph (229kph)

**NUMBER BUILT**  12,920

*"Anyone who can conquer its idiosyncrasies will find it an appealing machine. Others who can't may find the concentration required to drive it well inappropriate."*  ROAD TEST, *MOTOR* MAGAZINE, 1973

# COSTIN AMIGO

Frank Costin was an eccentric, chain-smoking engineer whose mastery of aerodynamics—gleaned in the aircraft industry—made him a godsend to racing teams like Lotus and Vanwall in the 1950s. He became the "-cos" part of sports car firm Marcos with partner Jem Marsh; his aeronautical engineering expertise led him to take the unusual step of using laminated marine plywood for the chassis of his first cars, to minimize weight.

Marcos eventually dropped this unique construction method but Frank Costin was convinced it had potential for further development. He eventually raised the finance to build his own wooden-chassis car. Perhaps understandably, the Costin Amigo looked vaguely like a Marcos 1800. It was built around a plywood monocoque frame, with pine strips bonded on to reinforce it, and fiberglass body panels for extreme lightness and a notably smooth finish.

The 121ci (1,975cc) engine, running gear, and suspension, came from the Vauxhall VX4/90. Frank Costin is said to have chosen this car after being impressed by a rented model. The Amigo was built in a small factory at an airfield near Vauxhall's Luton plant. Thanks to its low weight and highly aerodynamic shape, the Amigo gave a stunning performance from its rather unremarkable running gear. It could reach 137mph (220kph), and gained acclaim for its handling. This might have been compensation for the austere interior and £3,326 price, but only eight cars were sold.

## SPECIFICATION

**YEAR REVEALED** 1970

**PLACE OF ORIGIN** Little Staughton. Bedfordshire, UK

**HISTORICAL STATUS** production car

**ENGINE** four-cylinder, 121ci (1,975cc)

**MAXIMUM POWER** 96bhp

**LAYOUT** front-mounted engine driving the rear wheels

**BODYWORK** two-door, two-seater coupé

**TOP SPEED** 137mph (220kph)

**NUMBER BUILT** eight

*"Frank Costin was not a man to suffer half-baked projects gladly. He was a dedicated nonconformist, and more often than not he failed to receive the credit and recognition that were his due."*

OBITUARY OF FRANK COSTIN BY DAVID TREMAYNE, THE *INDEPENDENT* NEWSPAPER, 1995

The Costin Amigo offered a performance that belied its mundane drivetrain, thanks to close attention to its construction and streamlining.

# SOMMER JOKER

The car world went beach buggy crazy in the late 1960s, inspired by California's surf culture. A "different" contribution from cold, remote Denmark might have been expected, and the Joker didn't disappoint.

It came from the fertile mind of Danish car distributor Olé Sommer, who intended to offer a none-too-serious car that could be practical in the wild. His Joker rode on a stout box-section separate chassis on which an external framework of hot-dip galvanized steel pipes acted as the body frame. Between their gaps, on the inside, were attached totally flat fiberglass panels, giving the van-like Joker the appearance of a mobile farm building. "Doors" were canvas sidescreens, and the exhaust pipe transversed the car under the running board before exiting on the opposite side.

The mechanical parts were all Volvo, and being lightweight the Joker was said to have excellent acceleration. Seven examples were sold. Olé Sommer had been apprenticed at Jaguar before unexpectedly inheriting his late father's garage at just 21. He turned it into a large business, selling imported cars from Volvo and a variety of British marques.

## SPECIFICATION

**YEAR REVEALED**  1970

**PLACE OF ORIGIN**  Copenhagen, Denmark

**HISTORICAL STATUS**
production car

**ENGINE**  four-cylinder, 121ci (1,986cc)

**MAXIMUM POWER**  82bhp

**LAYOUT**  front-mounted engine driving the rear wheels

**BODYWORK**  door-less, four-seater station wagon

**TOP SPEED**  unknown

**NUMBER BUILT**  seven

*"Denmark is too small to support car manufacturing. Sweden has been just big enough to do it themselves, but Denmark? Only if the idea is sufficiently extreme."*

OLÉ SOMMER

Denmark's response to the buggy craze seemed to be made from a shed, rather than built in one, but was practical and robust.

# LAMBORGHINI COUNTACH

Lamborghini's Countach eclipsed even the company's earlier Miura model as the ultimate exotic sports car.

The Miura's voluptuous looks had caused a sensation in 1966, and now the Countach did it again. The car's designer, Marcello Gandini at Bertone, was the same, but the Miura was broader and flatter in character. The cab-forward racer look on the new design highlighted the fundamental difference between Miura and Countach. The sensational V12 engine was the same and still mid-mounted but, in the new car, it was now positioned in-line, with the gearbox located between the driver and the passenger seats.

Lamborghini badge

The 1971 LP500 show car, painted bright yellow, was the motoring pin-up of its time, with a 178mph (286kph) top speed. But changes were required before wealthy customers roared off in the first production version, named the LP400. In particular, the bodywork gained several prominent air ducts to ventilate the potent power unit.

The Countach would be on sale until 1990, but later cars, while gaining bigger engines, also had towering aerofoils, bulges to cover the six repositioned carburetors, extended wheelarches, and enormously fat tires. Ironically, the aerodynamic addenda increased the car's roadholding but blunted its top speed.

## SPECIFICATION

**YEAR REVEALED** 1971

**PLACE OF ORIGIN** Modena, Italy

**HISTORICAL STATUS**
production car

**ENGINE** V12-cylinder, 240–315ci
(3,929–5,167cc)

**MAXIMUM POWER** 455bhp
(5,167cc)

**LAYOUT** mid-mounted engine
driving the rear wheels

**BODYWORK** two-door,
two-seater coupé

**TOP SPEED** 178mph (286kph)

**NUMBER BUILT** 2,042

*"You seem to be lying down in the bottom of a light bulb, clutching this tacky black doughnut of a wheel, and trying to imagine yourself doing the best part of 200mph. What a car!"*

DOUG BLAIN, *CAR* MAGAZINE, 1974

The Countach made an enormous impact on 1970s car fanatics; this prototype shows the purity of line later lost to spoilers and wide wheels.

America put more than a man on the Moon—it put a car up there too, in the shape of the most expensive "Rover" of all time.

# NASA LUNAR ROVING VEHICLE

Four of these '"cars" were made, and for each minute they were driven for their intended purpose, they cost over $58,000.

NASA's Lunar Roving Vehicle ("LRV") was known as the Moon Buggy, and the most expensive "Rover" ever built! Maybe fittingly, Americans were the first to drive on the Moon. One LRV was even involved in a minor accident. When one of the Rover's fenders became detached, astronauts used tape to fix it back on, so severe was the dust cloud without it.

Wheeled-transport to give astronauts a wider Moon range was first envisaged in the early 1960s by NASA rocket scientist Dr. Wernher von Braun. In July 1969, two weeks before the epoch-making Apollo 11 mission, tenders to build a suitable vehicle were invited. The $19.6 million contract was won by Boeing and subcontractor General Motors, in time for Apollo 15 by April 1971.

The aluminum rover was compacted for the space journey, its wheels folding out in the automated unloading process. Its articulated chassis had front and rear steering for maximum maneuverability, and woven steel thread tires with titanium treads for best grip. Electric motors were fed by high-energy batteries. The LRV was controlled by a T-shaped joystick, and Velcro seatbelts were provided. The umbrella-like antenna beamed live footage back to Mission Control during the vehicles' sample- and data-gathering forays. Four LRVs were built and first drove on the Moon on July 31, 1971. Between them they covered 56 miles (90km),

## SPECIFICATION

**YEAR REVEALED** 1971

**PLACE OF ORIGIN** Kent, Washington

**HISTORICAL STATUS** quasi-production vehicle

**ENGINE** four electric motors

**MAXIMUM POWER** unknown

**LAYOUT** engines mounted in the wheel hubs driving all four wheels

**BODYWORK** doorless, single-seater buggy

**TOP SPEED** 8mph (13kph)

**NUMBER BUILT** four

*"Don't you worry about getting to the Moon—I will get you there. It's what you do when you get there that's important. You'll probably be driving a car on the Moon."*

SATURN V DESIGNER, WERNHER VON BRAUN

The LRVs were left behind on the lunar surface when the missions had been completed.

The prominent black plastic "bumpers" were meant to be kind to pedestrians, while ESV occupants enjoyed a cabin fortified against impacts.

# FIAT ESV 1500

The impetus for Fiat's attempt to create the safest possible city car came from the US. In 1970, the National Highway Safety Bureau announced its Experimental Safety Vehicle (ESV) project, to stimulate ideas for substantially safer cars to be on sale by 1980. Many carmakers responded with prototypes for evaluation: hardly altruistic—they were seeking favorable influence in the world's biggest car market.

Fiat's three-car contribution included this one, the world's first safety car weighing 1,500lb (680kg). Built between October 1971 and March 1972, the ESV 1500 featured a massively strong inner skeleton, with separate lateral structure and floor incorporated into a hefty box-type body frame. Cradled within was the standard mechanical hardware from a Fiat 500. The body used the Fiat 126's wheelbase and doors, and vaguely resembled the old Fiat 850. Its bizarre looks came from huge polyurethane cushion-type bumpers at either end with lights buried deep within them, protruding side bump strips in matching black plastic, and an obviously reinforced roof.

Fiat built 47 ESV prototypes. Thirteen of these were 1500s, and several were used in head-on crash test experiments, many at high speeds. However, with the fuel crisis panic of 1973, ESVs were sidelined, probably to Fiat's relief. The ESV 1500 would have been a marketing nightmare: its hefty weight called for a bigger, thirstier engine, and a higher price.

## SPECIFICATION

**YEAR REVEALED** 1972

**PLACE OF ORIGIN** Turin, Italy

**HISTORICAL STATUS** prototype

**ENGINE** two-cylinder, 36ci (594cc)

**MAXIMUM POWER** 18bhp

**LAYOUT** rear-mounted engine driving the rear wheels

**BODYWORK** two-door, four-seater sedan

**TOP SPEED** unknown

**NUMBER BUILT** 13

*"Should we ask ourselves if there is not a less onerous solution, one for instance linking the safe car to the safe road? Safety is based on a triangle whose three points are: man, the road, and the vehicle."*

OSCAR MONTABONE, HEAD OF FIAT RESEARCH AND DEVELOPMENT, SPEAKING
AT THE THIRD ESV CONFERENCE, WASHINGTON, US, 1972

Modified family cars, such as this Ford Escort RS Mk1, made rallying an extraordinary spectator sport, and more than proved their stamina.

A closely packed group of Dodge Daytonas, and a lone Ford, pound their way round the Daytona 500 race in Florida in 1970.

# ZAGATO ZELE 1000

Throughout the 1950s and 1960s, Italian coachbuilder Zagato was a byword for motoring excitement—a dream factory making strikingly styled sports cars. So no wonder visitors to the 1972 Geneva Motor Show were shocked at the company's display. It's new car was 77in (196cm) long, and could manage 25mph (40kph) in eerie silence.

The rationale for designing the Zele was straightforward: Zagato was in trouble, its traditional market for handmade Italian GT cars quickly eaten away by cheap rivals such as the Ford Capri, Opel Manta, and Datsun 240Z. Zele provided a new direction for the Italian company, founded in 1919.

The "1000" stood for the wattage available from its Marelli electric motor attached to the rear axle, fed by four 24-volt batteries.

It proved a prescient move because, by the time the boxy little Zele was rolling down Zagato's production line in Milan in 1974, the global fuel crisis spurred on by Middle East turmoil was biting hard. Alternative fuel vehicles were in vogue, and by 1975, Zele annual sales were 225. Zagato had distributors in the US (Elcar) and Britain (Bristol); a van and an open golf buggy, perfect for Florida, were developed by 1978, and the 1981 Nuova Zele offered four-seater accommodation.

Zagato continued to make electric cars until 1991, by which time the fortunes of its specialized car coachwork business had been revived thanks to exciting co-productions such as the Aston Martin Vantage Zagato and Alfa Romeo SZ.

## SPECIFICATION

**YEAR REVEALED** 1972

**PLACE OF ORIGIN** Milan, Italy

**HISTORICAL STATUS** production car

**ENGINE** electric motor

**MAXIMUM POWER** unknown

**LAYOUT** rear-mounted engine driving the rear wheels

**BODYWORK** two-door, two-seater sedan

**TOP SPEED** 25mph (40kph)

**NUMBER BUILT** approximately 3,000 (all Zagato electric vehicles)

*"If you need an extra spurt of power to cut off a pizza delivery boy, there's the overdrive pedal. Pressing it gives the Zele an extra but limited burst of speed. Since it's an electrical current that powers the engine and not gas, air, and a spark, like a light bulb it's either on or off, meaning the driver has little control."*

PAUL WALTON, *CLASSIC & SPORTS CAR* MAGAZINE, 2007

A world away from Zagato's sports car bodies, the upright electric Zele kept the company afloat through the grim economic 1970s wasteland.

With its huge expanse of glass and hatchback rear, the "compact" Pacer stood out to passers by; but its mechanical specification was compromised.

# AMC PACER

Caught out by the fuel crisis of the mid-1970s, US carmakers simply did not offer the right cars. They could only look on aghast as economical Japanese imports snatched their sales. The panic to compete sired some terrible emergency products, such as the Ford Pinto, which developed a tendency to catch fire in rear-end collisions. The AMC Pacer, meanwhile, took a more considered approach, but its fate was, sadly, overtaken by events.

"Project Amigo," begun in 1971, set out to create "the first Wide Small Car," keeping the roomy passenger compartment Americans liked but within a typical "European" length, and using a refined and compact Wankel rotary engine. It was also planned to exceed all anticipated safety requirements; hence, the goldfish-bowl-like glasshouse for optimum all-round visibility, the reinforced barrel-shaped flanks, and the rollover bar incorporated into the roof.

But things started to go wrong in 1974 when General Motors, scheduled to supply the power unit, axed its rotary engine program in the face of rocketing gas prices, reliability worries, and excessive emissions. American Motors was forced to install its own straight-six, a heavy, bulky, and inefficient engine, which would saddle the Pacer with mediocre performance and fuel economy. Novel touches such as a hatchback, and rack-and-pinion steering, helped sales in 1976 to top 117,000, but thereafter orders collapsed despite station wagon and V8 engine options.

## SPECIFICATION

**YEAR REVEALED** 1975

**PLACE OF ORIGIN** Kenosha, Wisconsin

**HISTORICAL STATUS** production car

**ENGINE** six-cylinder, 232/258ci (3,799/4,235cc) and V8-cylinder, 304ci 4, (980cc)

**MAXIMUM POWER** 130bhp

**LAYOUT** front-mounted engine driving the rear wheels

**BODYWORK** three-door, four-seater sedan and station wagon

**TOP SPEED** 104mph (167kph)

**NUMBER BUILT** 279,094

*"Bold, clean, and unique... even when it's going 60mph it still looks as if it's standing still! [The car's] engineering—old-fashioned and unimaginative in the extreme—does not match the perky design, which is most attractive to look at and pleasant to sit in."*

ROAD TEST, *ROAD & TRACK* MAGAZINE, 1975

# LEPOIX DING

The French-born industrial designer Louis Lepoix was probably best known for his commercial vehicles and household products through his consultancy Form Technic International. However, at the 1975 Frankfurt Motor Show he unveiled a pair of astonishing electric cars.

The Lepoix Shopi was, at first glance, a three-wheeler, although it actually had two tiny front wheels set close together. As the name implied, it was a 58in- (147cm-) long, golf-cart-like runabout intended for trips to local stores and, because it used a 24-volt electric motor fed by batteries, it was a zero-emissions vehicle.

However, while the Shopi was meant for mundane errands, the Lepoix Ding was outrageous and slightly baffling. Its molded plastic body and side-by-side seating were identical to the Shopi's but, instead of riding on a steel underframe, it was suspended from a stout, arched external chassis/rollcage, on the end of whose three "legs" was a bubble-formed wheel/tire.

The two passengers sat in the center while the driver stood up behind them, controlling the Ding using a tiller. It could buzz along much more swiftly than the Shopi, its electric motor allowing 16mph (26kph).

Alas, neither made it, despite sales being scheduled for a 1977 start. Instead, these vehicles acted as statements of Lepoix's passion for alternative fuel propulsion, alongside windmills and solar power. His output eventually ran to 3,000 designs—from cars to typewriters and parking meters.

## SPECIFICATION

**YEAR REVEALED** 1975

**PLACE OF ORIGIN** Baden-Baden, West Germany

**HISTORICAL STATUS** prototype

**ENGINE** electric motor

**MAXIMUM POWER** unknown

**LAYOUT** rear-mounted engine driving the rear wheels

**BODYWORK** doorless, two-seater-plus-standing-driver buggy

**TOP SPEED** 16mph (26kph)

**NUMBER BUILT** one

*"The author can only express his regret that the public was not ready for such a prodigy as the Lepoix Ding."*

CHRIS REES IN HIS BOOK *MICROCAR MANIA*, 1995

It almost defies description, but the Lepoix Ding, with its battery power, really could be driven—by someone standing at the back using a tiller.

Roger Moore as James Bond and the Lotus Esprit Turbo pose during filming of the 1981 movie *For Your Eyes Only*.

# LOTUS ESPRIT

No two-seater, mid-engined sports car in the world has had a longer life than the Esprit, on sale from 1976 to 2004. The car came about when Lotus founder Colin Chapman decided to update his Europa. But, instead of using his own stable of designers, Chapman chose a young Italian he met by chance, Giorgetto Giugiaro.

The result was low-slung and ultra-wedge-shaped, a racing car for the road that you had to be agile just to climb into. It was built around Lotus's famed "backbone" chassis, with the engine centrally located behind the driver's shoulders.

The prototype caused a sensation at the 1972 Turin Motor Show. The wider world, however, came to know the Esprit through the movies. In an astute "product placement" deal, Chapman persuaded producers of the James Bond films to feature his Esprit in the 1977 film *The Spy Who Loved Me*. Roger Moore's white example was as fast at sea as it was on the road, in one memorable scene being driven by Bond underwater—and, to the surprise of sunbathers, out on to the beach. Certainly, no real-life buyers could specify concealed missiles, periscope, or on-board radar. In fact, early "real" Esprits tended to overheat, vibrated horribly, and were judged claustrophobic and not especially rapid. Still, roadholding was never less than scintillating and by 1980, and the launch of the 152mph (245kph) Esprit Turbo, it was enormously improved. One year later and it also notched up its third James Bond outing.

## SPECIFICATION

**YEAR REVEALED** 1975

**PLACE OF ORIGIN** Hethel, Norfolk, UK

**HISTORICAL STATUS** production car

**ENGINE** four-cylinder, 120–133ci (1,973–2,174cc) and V8-cylinder, 214ci (3,506cc)

**MAXIMUM POWER** 350bhp

**LAYOUT** mid-mounted engine driving the rear wheels

**BODYWORK** two-seater coupé

**TOP SPEED** 175mph (282kph)

**NUMBER BUILT** 10,675

*"Apart from the astonishing roadholding, there is so much feel, via both the steering and the chassis, that even a very inexperienced driver is rarely likely to reach the car's exceptionally high cornering limits."*

ROAD TEST OF AN ESPRIT S3 IN *MOTOR* MAGAZINE, 1981

# ASTON MARTIN LAGONDA

Outsiders would never have guessed that the company behind the spectacular sedan pulling crowds ten-deep at the 1976 London Motor Show was on its knees. But Aston Martin was staring bankruptcy in the face in the spring of 1976 when, as a last-ditch attempt to save the company, its directors decided to create a four-door sedan to put even Rolls-Royce and Maserati in the shade for impact and sumptuousness.

Heroic work by stylist William Towns and engineering head Mike Loasby ensured the car was the motoring media event of the year. Although using reworked and lengthened Aston Martin V8 underpinnings, the relationship was far from obvious: the dramatic, sleek, wedge-shaped sedan was a world away from Aston's voluptuous curves.

Inside was an automotive breakthrough: the world's first car with a totally digital, touch-sensitive dashboard using LEDs and a microprocessor to activate controls. In truth, it was a somewhat premature use of the technology because the system proved difficult to perfect and unreliable to use. In 1984, the display was changed to cathode ray tubes, and later to fluorescent vacuum.

Despite taking 170 deposits at its Earl's Court unveiling, delays were emblematic of the Lagonda's hasty development. The first car wasn't delivered until 1979, by which time the price had risen to £32,000. Despite the teething problems, the Lagonda proved a strong seller, particularly in the Middle East. No doubt, too, it saved the great British Aston Martin marque from oblivion.

## SPECIFICATION

**YEAR REVEALED** 1976

**PLACE OF ORIGIN** Newport Pagnell, Buckinghmshire, UK

**HISTORICAL STATUS** production car

**ENGINE** V8-cylinder, 326ci (5,340cc)

**MAXIMUM POWER** 300bhp (Series 3, with fuel-injection)

**LAYOUT** front-mounted engine driving the rear wheels

**BODYWORK** four-door, four-seater sedan

**TOP SPEED** 145mph (233kph) (Series 2)

**NUMBER BUILT** 645

*"The Lagonda, low and lavish, was presented to a stunned public. Costing around £20,000, Aston Martin's new space-age Lagonda boasts 140mph performance from its 5.3-liter V8."*

AUTOCAR MAGAZINE, 1977

The four-door Lagonda was a last-ditch attempt to breathe new life into Aston Martin, and really astounded the motoring world.

# STIMSON SCORCHER

Britain's licensing authorities weren't too sure what to make of the Stimson Scorcher in 1976, hesitatingly classifying it as a motorcycle-sidecar combination.

By law, that meant "rider" and "pillion" had to wear crash helmets but the third occupant—the Scorcher seated three in a row—was legally the sidecar occupant and, thus, could ride bareheaded. However, designer Barry Stimson advised Scorcher occupants to all wear helmets because his outrageous trike, with British Leyland Mini subframe, engine, and gearbox at the front, could touch a daredevil 100mph (161kph).

The plastic body was made of fiberglass, and the engine was completely exposed, hot-rod style—unless you splurged on the optional plastic hood.

Mr. Stimson was a seminal figure on the burgeoning British kit car scene of the 1970s. His company Noovoh Developments sold the Scorcher as a self-assembly package, for £385, that could be carried home on a roof rack. Capable, enthusiastic mechanics could then build their own Scorcher using salvaged mechanical parts from a decrepit or crash-damaged Mini.

Stimson's initial kit car design was the Mini Bug of 1970 which became one of Britain's best-selling kit cars. New Stimson designs, however, soon followed, including the six-wheeled Safari Six, also relying on Mini parts, and then the Scorcher, of which a mere 30 were made in four years. Barry Stimson is in the kit car business to this day, and surviving Scorchers rarely change hands.

## SPECIFICATION

**YEAR REVEALED** 1976

**PLACE OF ORIGIN** Brighton, East Sussex, UK

**HISTORICAL STATUS** production car

**ENGINE** four-cylinder, 52–78ci (848–1,275cc)

**MAXIMUM POWER** up to 76bhp

**LAYOUT** front-mounted engine driving the front wheels

**BODYWORK** doorless, three-seater roadster

**TOP SPEED** 100mph (161kph)

**NUMBER BUILT** 30

*"It's the worst seller of all my cars, but the most famous—I find that weird. You either work to make a living by designing exactly what people want, or else you go a stage further by being a bit different and you have no market."* BARRY STIMSON, 2003, ON THE SCORCHER

This three-wheeled kit car from the fertile mind of Barry Stimson is a rare and sought-after beast—but it's hard to decide if it's car or motorbike.

Patrick Depailler putting the Tyrrell P34 through its paces on the Monaco Grand Prix circuit; note the small "window" for placing the six wheels.

# TYRRELL P34

The Tyrrell P34 was the boldest car seen on Formula One grids during the 1970s.

The idea of six wheels came from Derek Gardner, Tyrrell's chief designer, who calculated in 1974 that four small wheels at the front would hugely reduce a Formula One car's fontal area. Cutting aerodynamic drag would make the car faster, yet maintain the same surface-grip of two large wheels. For the P34, he chose 10in (25cm) diameter wheels, with crossply tires specially made by Goodyear. All four wheels were steered and were fitted with miniature disc brakes.

The car caused a storm when unveiled to the press in 1975, and made its public debut in the 1976 Spanish Grand Prix in the characteristic blue Elf oil livery. The P34 showed great promise, especially when Jody Scheckter won the 1976 Swedish Grand Prix driving a P34, and his team-mate Patrick Depailler brought his example home second.

Unfortunately, that was the pinnacle of success; this radical racer was dogged by braking and aerodynamics problems, and Goodyear had insufficient test facilities to develop the P34's tiny tires to keep abreast of the latest rubber technology.

The P34 saw no further wins, although it often finished second. It was campaigned throughout the 1977 season, constantly modified but progressively less competitive. To Derek Gardner's disappointment, the car was then retired as Tyrrell concentrated on the conventional 008 four-wheeler. Present Formula One regulations restrict cars to a four-wheeled layout only.

## SPECIFICATION

**YEAR REVEALED** 1976

**PLACE OF ORIGIN** Ockham, Surrey, UK

**HISTORICAL STATUS** Formula One racing car

**ENGINE** V8-cylinder, 183ci (2,993cc)

**MAXIMUM POWER** 485bhp

**LAYOUT** mid-mounted engine driving the rear wheels

**BODYWORK** single-seater racer

**TOP SPEED** 186mph (299kph)

**NUMBER BUILT** seven

*"When Ken Tyrrell rings you up and says: 'Can you come over, I've got something to show you', you don't ask: 'What?' or 'Why?'. After a welcoming cup of coffee, he said: 'Come out into the garden'. Totally unprepared for what to expect, I followed him out to the lawn and my mouth fell open, and a look of total disbelief came upon my face."*

DENIS "JENKS" JENKINSON, SAGE OF *MOTOR SPORT* MAGAZINE, ON FIRST SEEING THE P34

"Herbie", that loveable Volkswagen Beetle with a mind of its own, first starred in the 1968 Walt Disney movie *The Love Bug*. This huge-grossing family action-comedy produced four sequels during the 1970s and another over 30 years later in 2005. This still from *The Love Bug* includes a famous continuity goof—the car should have had a "53" roundel on the open door, too.

The entire body of the 79 was used as a vacuum to suck the car down on to the racetrack; this "Black Beauty" proved dominant on the F1 grid.

# LOTUS 79

Italian-American racing driver Mario Andretti declared the Lotus 78 drove "like it was painted to the road," and proved this Formula One car's uncanny winning streak by driving it to four victories in 1977. But after trying its successor, the 79 with 30 percent extra downforce, he declared the old car felt "like a London bus" by comparison. In 1978, the 79 helped him to the drivers' World Championship.

The Lotus 78 had pioneered "ground effect" aerodynamics in Formula One after Lotus founder Colin Chapman and his design team discovered that sidepods shaped like inverted aircraft wings could form venturi tunnels on either side of the narrow chassis. This created a vacuum that literally sucked the car on to the tarmac. Wind tunnel experiments using a rolling road produced amazing results, which were replicated on the test track using a stiff suspension to maintain a ground-hugging stance. Flexible, sliding rubber skirts stopped destabilizing air being drawn in from the sides.

The 79 brought a radical rethink. The whole car was now one giant "ground effect" venturi. The bodywork was extended back between the rear wheels, and the suspension redesigned, so that low pressure was evenly spread along the car's underside. This improved grip, and meant a relatively small rear aerofoil was required, causing less drag. The 79 was one of the most elegant Formula One designs ever; together with its John Player Special livery, this brought about its nickname of "Black Beauty".

## SPECIFICATION

**YEAR REVEALED** 1977

**PLACE OF ORIGIN** Hethel, Norfolk, UK

**HISTORICAL STATUS** Formula One racing car

**ENGINE** V8-cylinder, 183ci (2,993cc)

**MAXIMUM POWER** 480bhp

**LAYOUT** mid-mounted engine driving the rear wheels

**BODYWORK** single-seater racer

**TOP SPEED** approximately 180mph (289kph)

**NUMBER BUILT** six

*"In motor racing, Chapman had a place at the top; he changed the face of the contemporary racing car. Chapman wasn't really an inventor. He was, instead, a developer. Practically everything for which he is credited existed before he thought about it."*

JABBY CROMBAC, *AUTOCAR* MAGAZINE, 1996

# COPPER ELECTRIC RUNABOUT

With every dramatic surge in oil prices comes renewed interest in alternative fuels for cars; the intense focus on electric power by carmakers at the end of the first decade of the 21st century is nothing new.

There was wide interest in bringing small electric cars to the market in the late 1970s, as the recent fuel crisis receded but the world dipped into an economic recession and concerns mounted about urban air pollution. Many prototypes were demonstrated but this particular example hailed from an unusual source: America's Copper Development Association, an industry body devoted to promoting metals in industry.

Its Runabout, the sixth in a series of electric car prototypes started in 1970, was a rolling advert for copper, featuring it in the motor, cables, switches, winding mechanisms, wiring, and also in brake drums, brake tubing, and air lines.

The Runabout was reasonably normal-looking. A glass sunroof helped to ventilate the cramped interior, while the smooth-fronted nose had pedestrian-friendly concealed windshield wipers, and the plastic body featured a useful hatchback.

The car was claimed to have a range of 79 miles (127km), and running costs of no more than two cents a kilometer. Its 18 six-volt batteries could recharge overnight.

The copper industry was in the doldrums, and the lack of uptake in electric cars didn't help. But no-one could foresee the explosion in telecommunications and IT—consuming enormous amounts of copper.

## SPECIFICATION

**YEAR REVEALED** 1979

**PLACE OF ORIGIN** New York

**HISTORICAL STATUS** prototype

**ENGINE** electric motor

**MAXIMUM POWER** 14bhp

**LAYOUT** front-mounted engine driving the rear wheels

**BODYWORK** two-door, four-seater sedan

**TOP SPEED** 59mph (95kph)

**NUMBER BUILT** one

*"Designed specifically for the second car market, the new Copper Electric Runabout is described as a short but roomy vehicle with excellent maneuverability in traffic."*

PRESS RELEASE FROM THE COPPER DEVELOPMENT ASSOCIATION, 1979

The pull-out battery pack was inserted along the center of the car's underside.

This neat commuter car was an early recognition of slowly dwindling fossil fuels, but showed little concern for reducing consumption of metals.

# DELOREAN DMC-12

In 1974, US engineer and automotive executive John DeLorean set out to create an "ethical" sports car, shunning the cynical practices of General Motors, where he'd enjoyed a glittering career.

DeLorean chose Northern Ireland as the manufacturing base for this new enterprise, lured by nearly £40 million in British government regeneration funding.

The DeLorean DMC-12 itself was a very weird vehicle. Part of DeLorean's ethics was that, like the Porsche 911, pure engineering principles would prevail. It was to be a rear-engined two-seater with a plastic chassis. He gave the car "gullwing" doors and body panels in stainless steel. These couldn't rust and made a paintshop unnecessary. A Citroën rotary engine was proposed.

But in 1979, the DeLorean engineering development was assigned to Lotus, and the concept was watered down, losing the rotary engine and plastic frame. Under its shiny steel panels, the car became little more than a Lotus Esprit with a V6 Renault engine.

Production began in December 1980. In the US, its sole market, the hype was immense but the reality was dire. The car was underpowered, unexciting to drive, expensive at $25,000, and poorly built. Still, no one was prepared for DeLorean's insolvency in January 1982.

The venture eventually lost £77 million of British taxpayers' money. Later, it emerged that the disgraced DeLorean had conspired with Lotus executives to defraud the business of millions of pounds.

## SPECIFICATION

**YEAR REVEALED** 1979

**PLACE OF ORIGIN** Belfast, Northern Ireland, UK

**HISTORICAL STATUS** production car

**ENGINE** V6-cylinder, 174ci (2,849cc)

**MAXIMUM POWER** 130bhp

**LAYOUT** rear-mounted engine driving the rear wheels

**BODYWORK** two-door, two-seater coupé

**TOP SPEED** 121mph (195kph)

**NUMBER BUILT** 8,550

*"The five early cars we hammered about Northern Ireland were abysmally short of any commercial standard of acceptability."*

JOHN DELOREAN IN *CAR AND DRIVER* MAGAZINE, 1981

DeLorean wanted buyers' eyes to light up at his "ethical" DMC-12.

Italdesign's early styling prototype; the car would later gain huge fame in the *Back To The Future* movies.

John Weitz, in appropriately snappy racing goggles, puts his new baby through its paces at the Lime Rock racetrack on June 23, 1980.

# WEITZ X600

The late John Weitz was among the first men to appear on the International Best-Dressed List in 1967, one of many career highlights that appeared to make his an effortlessly glamorous life. Designer of men's casual clothes, author of best-selling novels, photographer, and ex-US Army Intelligence officer, he used to crisscross the planet presiding over his fashion business. Berlin-born, London-educated Weitz was a colorful character who couldn't fail to come up with a colorful car.

For the frame of his X600 roadster, he took the engine and subframe from a Chevrolet Camaro Z28 chassis and welded it into a bespoke chassis. The swoopy X600 was aluminum clothed and resembled an Austin-Healey 3000 crossed with the Batmobile (emulating the latter's glossy black paintwork with red highlights). Weitz was no shrinking violet; he relished driving his powerful Allard J2X Le Mans racer direct from the racetrack to dinner in the Hamptons, his tuxedo and dress shirt grubby from the journey.

He did the X600 design work in his office at 600 Madison Avenue, and a quarter-scale model was translated into the real thing by craftsmen working at Mallalieu, British artisan makers of vintage Bentley copies.

The finished X600 was then air-freighted back to New York and greeted by huge publicity. But when Mallalieu was wound up after its founder's death, the X600 was stymied, and the sole example wound up forgotten in a Cleveland aircraft museum.

## SPECIFICATION

**YEAR REVEALED** 1979

**PLACE OF ORIGIN** New York and Wootton, Oxfordshire, UK

**HISTORICAL STATUS** prototype

**ENGINE** V8-cylinder, 302ci (4,949cc)

**MAXIMUM POWER** unknown

**LAYOUT** front-mounted engine driving the rear wheels

**BODYWORK** two-door, two-seater roadster

**TOP SPEED** unknown

**NUMBER BUILT** one

*"It was a weird sensation to drive it the first time. I drove it in England for about 10 yards and then drove it here when it landed at Kennedy Airport. I drove it into New York. 'Hey, it's my own car!' It was weird."* INTERVIEW WITH JOHN WEITZ, *AUTOMOBILE* MAGAZINE, 1987

# 6

---

## 1980 ONWARD

# DRIVING IN A FASTER, CLEANER WORLD

The automobiles of 1980 are recognizably related to those on sale today. In its overall concept, the layout of the average family sedan has barely changed at all, despite the development of practical new body styles, such as the multi-passenger vehicle or the super-compact suburban runabout.

However, the systems within today's cars have benefited from three decades of sustained refinement by engineers and designers. Cars are almost unbelievably more efficient than in previous decades, as well as boasting vastly increased active

and passive safety to protect drivers and passengers. They also emit a tiny fraction of the harmful chemicals that were once an accepted by-product of mass car ownership.

Popular cars are as standardized as they ever were, with similar models created by manufacturers right around the globe. But that has been no bar to imaginative thinking, as this chapter amply proves. Meanwhile, the search for alternatives to oil is propelling automobile design ever further into the future, with advances in electric, hydrogen, and even solar power.

# LIGIER JS4

Guy Ligier—Formula One team owner, motorway construction tycoon, and confidante of French president François Mitterrand—was an outside bet as a provider of ultra-small cars for marginalized motorists. Yet in 1980, the Ligier JS4 became an instant best-seller in its class.

Such tiny cars, with either sub-3ci (50cc) gas engines or larger diesels, could be driven by anyone over 14 without a driver's license, tax, annual roadworthiness test, or even license plates. This gave them unique appeal to young people averse to scooters and mopeds, although actually the usual buyers were senior citizens.

Designed by Ligier's son Philippe and derived from the company's tractor cabs, its boxy body was made of steel rather than plastic, and it enjoyed the sophistication of four-wheel independent suspension. If one wheel came off, the car could still be driven on three, with its low center of gravity and carefully balanced wheelbase and track.

The two-stroke Motobecane moped engine, with automatic transmission, would never bestow high performance, but the huge windshield, fat tires, quad-headlamps, and matt black wheelarches and bumpers made it oddly handsome. The racing car heritage ("JS" in the title saluted Ligier's friend Jo Schlesser, the late Formula One driver) was another reason 1981 sales reached an amazing 6,941.

## SPECIFICATION

**YEAR REVEALED** 1980

**PLACE OF ORIGIN** Abrest, Vichy, France

**HISTORICAL STATUS** production car

**ENGINE** single-cylinder, 3ci (49.9cc)

**MAXIMUM POWER** 3.2bhp

**LAYOUT** mid-mounted engine driving the rear wheels

**BODYWORK** two-door, two-seater sedan

**TOP SPEED** 28mph (45kph)

**NUMBER BUILT** approx 25,000 (to 1987, including 125cc JS8 and diesel models)

*"This car from Ligier could be the slowest in the world. But then it hasn't been designed for motorway driving. It is one people will love or hate."*

ANNE HOPE, *PULSE* MAGAZINE, 1981

"The Ligier For Everyone" slogan aimed to cash in on the marque's Formula One cachet.

The tiny Ligier may have been suspiciously similar to a tractor cab on four small wheels, but it was a thrifty microcar that proved very popular.

With McLaren's MP4-1 1981 arrival on the Formula One scene, driver safety took a step forward, with an exploration of carbon fiber construction.

# MCLAREN MP4-1

This machine revolutionized Formula One. It opened a new chapter in construction methods by introducing carbon-fiber-composites (CFCs) to what was then a sceptical racing community.

Until the MP4, the first result of Ron Dennis's arrival at the hallowed McLaren team, Formula One car chassis were built from aluminum—up to 50 different sections in a typical monocoque. The MP4, however, used just five carbon fiber moldings in a design conceived by free-thinking chief designer John Barnard and produced in the US by Hercules Aerospace.

The carbon fiber proved hugely stronger than metal, the stresses being fed along the axis of the strands. It was hard for seasoned engineers, used to working with metal alone, to grasp. But the driver safety inherent in this stiffer material was obvious after John Watson's MP4 was nearly destroyed in a crash at the 1981 Italian Grand Prix– he walked away largely unscathed. Hercules Aerospace still has the wreck to show its clients. Teammate Andrea De Cesaris also survived over 20 accidents in 1981 alone.

The MP4-1 made a good start in 1981, Watson winning the British Grand Prix; the MP4-1/B got into its stride with four victories in 1982, before the MP4-1/C became less competitive in 1988. Today's Vodafone McLaren Mercedes MP4-23 cars trace their roots directly back to the MP4-1, but so can every car on the Formula One grid—CFC is now the standard construction material.

## SPECIFICATION

**YEAR REVEALED**  1981

**PLACE OF ORIGIN**  Woking, Surrey, UK

**HISTORICAL STATUS**  Formula One racing car

**ENGINE**  V8-cylinder, 183ci (2,993cc)

**MAXIMUM POWER**  495bhp

**LAYOUT**  mid-mounted engine driving the rear wheels

**BODYWORK**  single-seater racer

**TOP SPEED**  200mph+ (322kph+ )

**NUMBER BUILT**  seven

*"A composite carbon fiber chassis was a big step into the unknown. The question all Formula One drivers were asking was: what was going to happen in an accident? Fortunately, the design turned out to be virtually bulletproof... The MP4-1 was born out of incredible vision."*

FORMULA ONE DRIVER JOHN WATSON ON THE MP4-1 IN *RACING LINE* MAGAZINE, 2006

# GENERAL MOTORS LEAN MACHINE

If you've seen the 1993 futuristic-action movie *Demolition Man*, you might be familiar with General Motors' Lean Machine.

It was created by GM's Frank Winchell, as a study for a single-seater commuter vehicle—car-like in use and stability, but offering motorcycle dimensions and maneuverability.

So the narrow Lean Machine had a fixed lower "power pod" section with two rear wheels, but a single wheel leading a separate upper "passenger pod" that pivoted from side to side in corners so the driver could lean into them like a biker. The ovular Lean Machine was compact and weather-proof, and the second of two versions built was said to reach 60mph (97kph) from standstill in 6.8 seconds.

Inside, it sported handlebar controls, with throttle and brakes also hand-operated. The angle of lean, however, was controlled by pedals. The Lean Machine was never a likely candidate for showrooms, despite General Motors' insistence that they considered it in 1989 for possible marketing in congested California. Its star turn came alongside 16 other GM concept cars, valued at $69 million, in *Demolition Man*.

## SPECIFICATION

**YEAR REVEALED** 1982

**PLACE OF ORIGIN** Detroit, Michigan

**HISTORICAL STATUS** prototype

**ENGINE** V2-cylinder, 46ci (750cc)

**MAXIMUM POWER** 30bhp

**LAYOUT** rear-mounted engine driving the rear wheels

**BODYWORK** single-canopy, single-seater sedan

**TOP SPEED** unknown

**NUMBER BUILT** two

*"One possibly historic innovation has been dubbed the 'Lean Machine' because of its slender girth and leaning capabilities. It may be the first new road vehicle invented this century."*

DESCRIPTION GIVEN AT GM "WORLD IN MOTION" EXHIBITION, WALT DISNEY WORLD, 1983

The power pod carried the Honda engine and two wheels, while the passenger pod and front wheel gave the machine its lean.

# RANGE ROVER "POPEMOBILE"

Transport for the pope during public appearances had tended to be in open limousines until the terrible event that befell Pope John Paul II on May 13, 1981. While blessing worshipers in St. Peter's Square, he was shot by a gunman only 15ft (4.5m) away. It was felt that any future vehicle carrying the pontiff must be bulletproof, and the first one so equipped was a Range Rover specially built for his British visit in summer 1982.

Naturally, it gained the popular moniker of "Popemobile" and the familiar image of a white vehicle with a towering glass box at the back for his Holiness became readily associated with it. However, the first such vehicle was actually built in 1980 for a trip to Germany, and based on a Mercedes-Benz G-Wagen. The 1982 Popemobile, therefore, continued the tradition of the host nation providing transport. British Leyland was obliged to help, and prevailed upon Ogle Design to oversee planning and construction.

Two identical Range Rovers were built at the insistence of security chiefs, equipped with run-flat tires and police radios. A rear door opened into a leather-upholstered interior, with four seats, that was also tall enough for the pope to stand up. Bulletproof glass extended only to "heart" level, and open side windows at the top meant he could be seen unobscured. Happily, no attempts were made on the pope's life during his tour; and he was just as secure in an enormous Leyland T45 Popemobile truck built for the Scottish leg. Afterwards, one of the Range Rovers was acquired by the Vatican.

## SPECIFICATION

**YEAR REVEALED** 1982

**PLACE OF ORIGIN** Solihull, West Midlands, and Letchworth, Hertfordshire, UK

**HISTORICAL STATUS** custom parade vehicle

**ENGINE** V8-cylinder, 215ci (3,525cc)

**MAXIMUM POWER** 132bhp

**LAYOUT** front-mounted engine driving all four wheels

**BODYWORK** three-door, six-seater station wagon

**TOP SPEED** unknown

**NUMBER BUILT** two

The Leyland truck Popemobile dwarfs the Range Rover.

*"[The clergy] had to negotiate with car companies for the manufacture of a right-hand-drive Popemobile. Amateurs though they were, they turned out to be very good."*

CLIFFORD LONGLEY WRITING IN *THE TABLET*, 1999, ON THE POPE'S VISIT TO THE UK

The British-made Popemobile was the first with bullet-proof glass, although part of the side windows was left open for a clear view of the pontiff.

Millions watched Africar prototypes on an epic journey in a TV documentary, but the venture to supply them for the Third World ended in chaos.

# AFRICAR

The Africar saga is a sorry and twisted tale of high ideals, financial chaos, and technical incompetence. But it's also the story of a fascinating project that promised cars tailor-made for Third World drivers.

Anthony Howarth was an Oscar-nominated documentary filmmaker whose assignments took him to poverty-stricken outposts. He'd noticed that mainstream vehicles built in developed countries often couldn't handle primitive roads, and in 1981, he resolved to create one that could.

To achieve this, his Africar had an abnormally wide track so it could surmount rutted dirt-tracks, aided by 12in- (30cm-) high ground clearance and soft Hydragas-damped suspension for a huge vertical wheel movement range. The bodywork was of plywood soaked in epoxy resin with fiberglass reinforcements, building toward Howarth's vision of franchized local manufacture with minimal capital investment. Power came from front-wheel drive Citroën 2CV mechanicals.

Three such prototypes completed an 18,000-mile (28,968-km) excursion from the Arctic Circle to the Equator. Howarth filmed the adventure for a memorable UK TV series, and orders consequently poured in.

This basic concept worked but, with the 2CV and its engine soon to be axed, Howarth tried to design his own. This engineering was way beyond him (and his budget), yet he still accepted deposits for cars—talking grandly of production plants from Bangladesh to Botswana. By 1988, Africar was bankrupt.

## SPECIFICATION

**YEAR REVEALED** 1983

**PLACE OF ORIGIN** Lancaster, Lancashire, UK

**HISTORICAL STATUS** prototype

**ENGINE** flat-two-cylinder, 37ci (602cc)

**MAXIMUM POWER** 29bhp

**LAYOUT** front-mounted engine driving the front wheels

**BODYWORK** two-door, three-seater utility; four-door, six-seater station wagon; others proposed

**TOP SPEED** 70mph (113kph)

**NUMBER BUILT** five

*"Henry Ford had the right idea. He was really setting up his mass-production methods in a Third World country. In 1920, the USA was vast and under-developed, and there was no public transport outside the cites."*

TONY HOWARTH INTERVIEWED IN *THE SUNDAY TIMES MAGAZINE*, 1986

# GLENFROME FACET

Meet the "Ultimate All-Terrain Sports Coupé." There had never been such a car until Glenfrome Engineering revealed its Facet, and proved off-road driving and Lamborghini-esque styling could mix.

The running gear was a standard Range Rover chassis, on which Glenfrome's coachbuilders created the chiseled-looking body. Windshield and door frames were aluminum castings, a tubular steel rollcage enclosed the four-seater cabin, and body panels were fiberglass. A neat touch was a lift-out Targa roof panel that slid into a storage compartment under the sloping, high-set hood; like the retractable rear window, this was power-operated. Rugged crash bars front and rear would ward off obstacles.

The design work came from Dennis Adams (normally associated with Marcos sports cars), and the manufacturer was a specialist in Range Rover conversions. The Facet was aimed squarely at Middle East nobility, where automotive one-upmanship knew no bounds. Glenfrome was among numerous British companies offering bespoke cars based on Range Rovers, loved for their desert capability, and the Facet was more extreme than most. Among myriad options, owners could request a handy winch discreetly concealed behind the front number plate. Prices were vast, but an agreement with American Express meant the car could be paid for on "plastic." Glenfrome converted 400 cars a year at one point, but was bankrupt by 1986.

## SPECIFICATION

**YEAR REVEALED** 1983

**PLACE OF ORIGIN** Solihull, West Midlands, and Bristol, UK

**HISTORICAL STATUS** production car

**ENGINE** V8-cylinder, 215ci (3,528cc)

**MAXIMUM POWER** 132bhp

**LAYOUT** front-mounted engine driving all four wheels

**BODYWORK** two-door, four-seater coupé

**TOP SPEED** unknown

**NUMBER BUILT** approximately 30

"*A lot of amused interest was created at the 1983 Motorfair exhibition in London by the Facet. It emphasizes the extraordinary versatility of the Range Rover that such a vehicle should be designed and produced, albeit at a formidable price of around £55,000.*"

STUART BLADON IN HIS BOOK *THE RANGE ROVER COMPANION*, 1984

Besides its extremely unusual lines, the Facet offered a removable roof panel that could be stored under its electrically operated hood.

With admirable Swedish logic, Saab used the EV-1 as the opportunity to create an advanced but fully working research car using 900 Turbo parts.

# SAAB EV-1

There's a vast array of designs that might illustrate the concept car boom of the 1980s, when manufacturers wanted to demonstrate their capabilities of the near- to medium-term future.

And almost all of them are empty vessels, dramatic yet delicate mock-ups with no chance of ever leaving the motor show hall. In this company, then, Saab's Experimental Vehicle No 1 (EV-1) was rather special: a fully working car brought from paper to reality in six months, and with the world's first automotive solar panels.

It was built by a team whose leader, Bjorn Envall, had masterminded Saab's styling since 1969. As brand new cars were a rarity from the Swedish manufacturer, he could give his stylists and engineers their head

with this purposeful-looking, wind-cheating sports car. The steel body had a fully-glazed bronze-tinted glasshouse with 66 solar cells, capturing ultraviolet rays to power the car's air-conditioning and keep the cockpit cool. Front and rear body sections were of Aramid composite, which regained its shape after dents, while the seats, adapted from a Chevrolet Corvette's, were 50 percent lighter than Saab's normal ones but incorporated powered side bolster supports.

The EV-1 boasted huge performance from the Saab 900 Turbo 16 engine, but it had to be safe, too. The doors had side impact bars incorporating carbon fiber layers. Tiny elliptic reflector headlamps provided blazing nighttime illumination, while the after-dark speedometer just lit the current speed range.

## SPECIFICATION

**YEAR REVEALED** 1985

**PLACE OF ORIGIN** Trollhättan, Sweden

**HISTORICAL STATUS** prototype

**ENGINE** four-cylinder, 121ci (1,985cc)

**MAXIMUM POWER** 285bhp

**LAYOUT** front-mounted engine driving the front wheels

**BODYWORK** two-door, four-seater coupé

**TOP SPEED** 169mph (272kph)

**NUMBER BUILT** one

*"The EV-1 can accommodate four adults and a vast amount of luggage. The latter is unusual on this type of car."*    BJORN ENVALL, HEAD OF THE EV-1 DESIGN TEAM

A genuine innovation on the EV-1 was these solar panels to power the air-conditioning.

# SINCLAIR C5

Consumer electronics tycoon Sir Clive Sinclair had long considered making silent, emissions-free electric vehicles. In August 1983, new rules came into force allowing "electrically assisted cycles" to hit the road with no driver's license, tax, insurance, or even helmet needed; they simply had to weigh under 132lb (60kg) and not exceed 15mph (24kph). Sinclair saw his chance, recognising that nothing prevented such a vehicle from being a tricycle.

After selling shares in Sinclair Research to raise funds of £12 million, he formed Sinclair Vehicles, and hired Lotus to coordinate the engineering. It required a new 12-volt deep discharge lead-acid battery, and a small Italian electric motor. Handlebars mounted under the rider's thighs were for steering.

The low-drag, upper body was remarkable: the largest single plastic injection-molding ever offered in a consumer product.

Christened the Sinclair C5, it was launched in London on January 10, 1985, at £428, including mail-order delivery. However, the C5 rolled into immediate controversy. Safety campaigners condemned it as unsafe and—in the British climate— uncomfortable. Some jibes were unfair, however; it didn't have a washing-machine engine despite being assembled by Hoover, and was a bicycle or moped alternative, not a surrogate car. Manufacture stopped in August 1985, and Sinclair Vehicles went into receivership afterward. The C5's failure scuppered a whole range of planned Sinclair electric vehicles.

## SPECIFICATION

**YEAR REVEALED** 1985

**PLACE OF ORIGIN** Warwick, Warwickshire, and Merthyr Tydfil, South Wales, UK

**HISTORICAL STATUS** production "car"

**ENGINE** electric motor

**MAXIMUM POWER** unknown

**LAYOUT** rear-mounted engine driving one rear wheel

**BODYWORK** doorless/open, single-seater buggy

**TOP SPEED** 15mph (24kph)

**NUMBER BUILT** approximately 12,000

*"Because of our work at Sinclair Research, the electronic control system is very advanced and we have a custom chip that monitors everything and controls everything... By encouraging people to be on three wheels rather than two we will be adding considerably to safety on the road."*

SIR CLIVE SINCLAIR, SPEAKING AT THE C5'S LAUNCH, 1985

Condemned as dangerous by critics, the Sinclair C5 was never really meant to be a car—more an "electrically assisted bicycle."

# ITALDESIGN AZTEC

Italdesign's Aztec 1988 show car was built around a gloriously pointless feature: twin cockpits for driver and passenger. Like the Asgard people-carrier and the Aspid coupé, it used mid-mounted Audi's turbocharged five-cylinder engines, transversely mounted, and Quattro four-wheel drive. But the Aztec's mad appeal of driver and passenger independently experiencing the rush of air was irresistible. Spoken communication was only possible through headsets, although the twin cockpits were linked at elbow level so the center console could be shared.

Italdesign driving force Giorgetto Giugiaro, normally a purveyor of neat, sensible styling for family cars like the Volkswagen Golf/Rabbit and Fiat Panda, gave the Aztec weird "service center" panels on both flanks around the rear wheelarch. They included coded door locks, controls to operate the inbuilt hydraulic jacks, digital engine fluid monitors, and separate compartments containing flashlight, fire extinguisher, and gas flap.

Was this arresting automotive another flash-in-the-pan? So it seemed, until Japanese entrepreneurs identified a market for a real Aztec, and acquired production rights. In 1991, a limited series of 50 faithful replicas was built. The bodies were made in Italy, and the cars taken to Germany to be fitted with Audi engines tuned by specialist Mayer MTM, before heading for Japan. Such unusual fun was hugely costly—each model was priced at $225,000. Still, Giorgetto Giugiaro signed each car before delivery.

## SPECIFICATION

**YEAR REVEALED** 1988

**PLACE OF ORIGIN** Turin, Italy

**HISTORICAL STATUS** prototype/ production car

**ENGINE** five-cylinder, 136ci (2,226cc)

**MAXIMUM POWER** 197/250bhp

**LAYOUT** mid-mounted engine driving all four wheels

**BODYWORK** two-door/two-canopy, two-seater roadster

**TOP SPEED** 150mph (241kph) (production model)

**NUMBER BUILT** 1/50

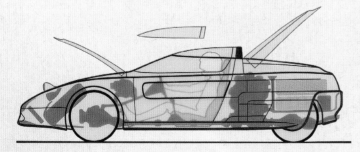

*"It is a great joy... that my original design has finally come to life as such a handcrafted masterpiece."*

GIORGETTO GIUGIARO, 1991

This Italdesign side view shows how engine and four-wheel drive fitted.

This overhead view shows the twin cockpits to great effect; no one thought the car would ever hit the road, but the Japanese had other ideas.

# MERCEDES-BENZ F 100

Since the 1950s, Mercedes-Benz cars had tended toward costliness, but the upside for buyers—aside from fastidious build quality—was a reassuring cocktail of safety and innovation. The F 100 research car provided all of this and more, with most of the nascent ideas packed into it, now adopted by mainstream models. It could never be described as pretty, but even its people-carrier profile is now commonplace.

Its only dead-end feature was the central driving position, for which Mercedes had provided immense "exploding" doors that took a chunk of the floor away when they opened. The F 100 was front-wheel drive—a Merc first—and its key structural feature was its sandwich floor and sloping bulkhead firewall shape, which would force the engine underneath the passenger compartment in a front-end collision. This arrangement appeared on the A-Class six years later.

But in the area of safety the F 100 was a true standard-bearer of future trends. The doors were opened by credit-type card that readied the driving position to the driver's pre-set ideal. The steering wheel featured voice activation and a keypad. The F 100 used a frontal radar-based system to maintain a safe distance from the vehicle in front; under the Distronic name, this arrived on the S-Class, in 1998. A pop-up video camera relaying its view to the in-dash screen for easy reversing hasn't featured yet, but rain-sensing windshield wipers and electronic tire pressure monitors arrived on Mercedes cars in 1995 and 1999 respectively.

## SPECIFICATION

**YEAR REVEALED** 1991

**PLACE OF ORIGIN** Stuttgart, Germany

**HISTORICAL STATUS** prototype

**ENGINE** six-cylinder, 158ci (2,597cc)

**MAXIMUM POWER** 194bhp

**LAYOUT** front-mounted engine driving the front wheels

**BODYWORK** four-door, five-seater station wagon

**TOP SPEED** unknown

**NUMBER BUILT** one

*"The F 100 concept represented a new research area for Mercedes-Benz: the minivan market. The driver sat dead-center front, followed by two rows of seats. Even the color—purple—was a fresh attempt for the German make."*

GREGORY JANICKI IN HIS BOOK *CARS EUROPE NEVER BUILT*, 1992

Mercedes-Benz used the nascent people-carrier as a canvas on which to paint its high-tech vision of the future, most of which has come to pass.

Sports cars under construction in the Worcestershire, UK, factory of Morgan, where handmade ash wood frames carry hand-formed steel panels.

In the Merseyside, UK, plant building Vauxhall Astras, human beings are absent in the bodyshop, where cars are welded together entirely by robots.

The burly form of the Hummer; about 1,000 of these massive vehicles were sold annually for 14 years, trading off their military image.

# AM GENERAL HUMMER

For the first Hummer, parallels with the original Willys Jeep are relevant: the company behind it, AM General, was the outfit that formerly made military Jeeps. The vehicle was meticulously planned to the US Army's brief for the ultimate go-anywhere machine that could be specified in several variations and resist anything thrown at it. It didn't have to be that fast; just unstoppable. The 1979 blueprint classified it as a "High Mobility Multi-purpose Wheeled Vehicle." Within 15 months, working prototypes were being appraised, and satisfied Army chiefs placed an order worth $1.2 billion for 55,000 "HMMWV's or "Humvees" in 1983. As the vehicles entered service, troops nicknamed them "Hummers". The underpinnings called for a ladder-frame separate chassis so it could be configured as anything—from troop carrier, to mini-tank, to ambulance—and independent suspension, by wishbones and coil springs, for towering ground clearance and wheel articulation.

The 1991 Gulf War was the Hummer M996's public launch TV advertising campaign, as the world watched the 396ci (7,483cc) monsters liberating Kuwait from Iraqi invasion. In 1992, a civilian model was introduced. It had a 378ci (6,200cc) diesel V8, but a detuned Chevrolet Corvette gas V8 was briefly offered in 1995. It cost up to $45,000 and came in four body configurations, designed specifically for off-road driving—conducting this behemoth along any highway was tricky.

## SPECIFICATION

**YEAR REVEALED**  1992

**PLACE OF ORIGIN**  South Bend, Indiana

**HISTORICAL STATUS**  military vehicle-derived production car

**ENGINE**  V8-cylinder, diesel 378–396ci (6,200-6,483cc); V8-cylinder, gas 350ci (5,735cc)

**MAXIMUM POWER**  195bhp

**LAYOUT**  front-mounted engine driving all four wheels

**BODYWORK**  four-door, five-seater station wagon or convertible (others offered)

**TOP SPEED**  87mph (140kph)

*"These are no ordinary Hummers. I had General Motors customize one of them into a hydrogen Hummer... I had another converted from diesel to biofuel. But now that I am governor,... my Hummers are usually in the garage."*

ARNOLD SCHWARZENEGGER, GOVERNOR OF CALIFORNIA AND HUMMER OWNER, TALKING TO GERMAN MAGAZINE *DER SPEIGEL*, 2007

With its four-wheel drive, rugged construction, and adjustable height, the Hobbycar was meant to be as useful on road as it was enjoyable in water.

# HOBBYCAR

This car brought the amphibious concept right up-to-date in 1992 in a vehicle bristling with novel design touches. It made a real splash on a spectacular stand at the Paris Motor Show that year.

Unlike the Amphicar (see pages 206–207), the Hobbycar was mid-engined rather than front-engined, for better on-water balance, and had four-wheel drive instead of two. The steel-reinforced fiberglass bodywork was also watertight, there being no doors for water to seep through. The four pivoting seats could be configured in numerous ways or folded down flush and locked shut, and the dashboard and steering column were also retractable and lockable as one unit. The windshield was retractable, electrically, to make the Hobbycar absolutely wide open.

Propulsion in the water was by two joystick-operated hydrojets that together gave 661lb (300kg) of thrust, for five-knot paddling. To cut water-resistance, the wheels could be pulled up inside the body. A Peugeot turbodiesel engine was the power source, and the car had adjustable hydro-pneumatic suspension settings for different terrain.

The Hobbycar seemed a neatly-resolved design, and the factory even had its own lake for potential buyers to test the car. Its makers sought to spread the risk of manufacturing expensive $45,000 playthings by developing a compact and luxurious family car, the Passport. This seemed to be a wise strategy, but when the company's resources became overstretched it was soon forced into administration.

## SPECIFICATION

**YEAR REVEALED**  1992

**PLACE OF ORIGIN**  Thenay, Loire, France

**HISTORICAL STATUS**  production car

**ENGINE**  four-cylinder, 116ci (1,905cc)

**MAXIMUM POWER**  92bhp

**LAYOUT**  mid-mounted engine driving all four wheels

**BODYWORK**  door-less, four-seater convertible buggy

**TOP SPEED**  87mph (140kph) on land five knots on water

**NUMBER BUILT**  52

*"Hobbycar offers a multitude of driving experiences in a single, infinitely convertible automobile… test drives [are available] on the track or the lake."*

FROM A HOBBYCAR BROCHURE, 1992

The Hobbycar could manage five knots and sported joystick-operated hydrojets.

The F1 undergoes tests on the MIRA circuit in Warwickshire, UK, prior to its launch on to the world stage, where it was the fastest car for a decade.

# MCLAREN F1

Gordon Murray enjoyed the rare privilege of building a pure supercar, no-expense-spared, with the McLaren F1. The ultimate roadgoing machine of its day, it remained the world's fastest production car for ten years.

Murray's background as chief Formula One designer at Brabham, then McLaren, left him with a burning passion to build a road car. His vision called for the fastest, most involving road car ever, yet also one you could happily drive into the city center.

Ideas at McLaren crystallized during 1988, and in March 1989, Murray formally announced his plans. He would be heading design and development, Lotus stylist Peter Stevens would pen the car's shape, and BMW Motorsport agreed to furnish a custom-made V12 engine.

Everything revolved around Murray's ideals, such as the three-seater cabin with the driver sitting centrally ahead of two passengers, and the world-first use of a carbon fiber composite monocoque.

Weight was crucial to the anticipated performance: an unbelievable 1 ton (1,000kg). With 627bhp on tap, the performance Murray wanted was made real. Formula One driver Jonathan Palmer drove one at Italy's Nardo test track in August 1993 to an incredible 231mph (372kph).

Such performance made the F1 invincible—an F1 GTR came first in every endurance race they entered, bar two, while the F1 was triumphant at Le Mans in 1995. The 635,000 price reflected development costs and the 6,000 man hours they took to build.

## SPECIFICATION

**YEAR REVEALED**  1992

**PLACE OF ORIGIN**  Woking, Surrey, UK

**HISTORICAL STATUS**  production car

**ENGINE**  V12-cylinder, 370ci (6,064cc)

**MAXIMUM POWER**  627bhp

**LAYOUT**  mid-mounted engine driving the rear wheels

**BODYWORK**  two-door, three-seater coupé

**TOP SPEED**  231mph (372kph)

**NUMBER BUILT**  107 in total including prototypes and racing editions

*"The F1 is the finest driving machine yet built for use on the public road."*

FROM THE ONLY FULL ROAD TEST EVER CONDUCTED OF AN F1,
*AUTOCAR* MAGAZINE, 1994

Although intended as a road car, racing was inevitable, and led to victory at Le Mans.

# RENAULT ZOOM

The chaotic free-for-all that is parking in Paris has often provided inspiration to French car designers. In the 1950s, for example, the little Reyonnah tandem car had wheels on outriggers that could be folded inward so it could occupy parking spaces little wider than a motorbike's.

The same set of issues lit up Renault's corporate imagination in 1992, for the Zoom, an electric city runabout. This time the trick was in its wheelbase. It was shrinkable, electrically, from its normal driving length of 8.7ft (265cm) to just 7.5ft (230cm) so that the Zoom could be squeezed into the most impossibly tight downtown spots. With its central pinch point, the car's height would grow from 4.9ft (149.5cm) to 5.7ft (172.5cm) as it tucked its rear end underneath to compact itself. The width remained constant at 5ft (152cm), and access was via two rotating doors that opened in the style of beetle wings.

The feather-light plastic body was easy for the 25kw electric motor (90 percent recyclable, Renault said) fed by nickel-cadmium batteries to propel, which endowed it with a range of 90 miles (145km) between recharges. The cheeky cabin design strongly evoked the Smart City-Coupé which would emerge several years later, and included a putative sat-nav system. However, Renault was also in the throes of launching its own new small car, the Twingo, a conventional gas model. The Zoom, co-designed with aerospace group Matra, is now just another step in Renault's varied concept car line-up.

## SPECIFICATION

**YEAR REVEALED** 1992

**PLACE OF ORIGIN** Paris, France

**HISTORICAL STATUS** prototype

**ENGINE** electric motor

**MAXIMUM POWER** 25kw

**LAYOUT** rear-mounted engine driving the rear wheels

**BODYWORK** two-door, two-seater sedan

**TOP SPEED** 75mph (121kph) (claimed)

**NUMBER BUILT** one

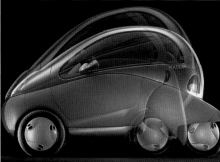

*"Even at lunchtime, one third of all cars on the roads in Paris are looking to park. You can see the benefits of perpendicular parking; [Zoom is] no bigger than a good armchair."*

AUTOCAR & MOTOR MAGAZINE, 1992

The Zoom could reduce its length by 14in (35cm) to squeeze into tight parking spaces.

The Zoom could have been an icon of the lack-of-space age, especially because its low-emission electric engine made it city-friendly.

# GM EV1

Across America, evidence that the EV1 was once the most forward-thinking car on sale is elusive; none are owned by private drivers, and even the few EV1s displayed in museums and institutes cannot function.

In 1996, the EV1 was the boldest electric car venture yet undertaken by a US carmaker, and the first mainstream car designed to run exclusively on batteries. At first, these were traditional lead-acid units offering a 75-mile (121-km) range at most, but a 1999 second-generation EV1 switched to nickel-metal hydride batteries, boosting range to 150 miles (241km). Regenerative braking perked up charge on the move.

General Motors built the EV1 to exploit the California Air Resources Board's 1990 "Zero-Emission Vehicle" (ZEV) mandate, which decreed that by 2003, 10 percent of all cars sold in the state must be emissions-free to alleviate chronic pollution. They were so tailor-made for sunshine states—California, Arizona, and Georgia—that cold weather meant EV1s could suffer elsewhere.

Rather than sell the cars direct, EV1s were leased to selected customers, who paid up to $549 a month. Users were hugely enthusiastic about the plastic-bodied two-seater, which was smooth and quiet. It's also the most aerodynamic car ever marketed, with a drag coefficient of 0.19. However, by 2004, and with all leases expired, General Motors destroyed the bulk of EV1s; it claimed the car was hugely loss-making, risked liabilities, and amended environmental laws made it redundant.

## SPECIFICATION

**YEAR REVEALED** 1996

**PLACE OF ORIGIN** Lansing, Michigan

**HISTORICAL STATUS**
production car

**ENGINE** electric motor

**MAXIMUM POWER** 137bhp
equivalent

**LAYOUT** front-mounted engine
driving the front wheels

**BODYWORK** two-door,
two-seater coupé

**TOP SPEED** 80mph (129kph)

**NUMBER BUILT** 1,117

*"Certainly when you put your foot down in an EV1, the fun of the snappy acceleration is slightly spoilt by the sight of the charge indicator heading for zero."* THE ECONOMIST MAGAZINE , 1996

The EV1, with a drag coefficient of just 0.19, is the world's slipperiest production car; this special four-seater model remained a one-off.

In the back of the Life-Jet was a 98ci (1,598cc) Mercedes A-Class engine powering the rear wheel; the roof could also be stowed for sunny days.

# MERCEDES-BENZ F 300 LIFE-JET

Carmakers have long shunned the idea of offering three-wheeled cars to their customers. Motorcycle manufacturers never promote anything that detracts from pure, two-wheeled excitement. But for flights of creative fantasy, three-wheeled machines mixing car and bike get plenty of attention, and this one from Mercedes-Benz packed a real technological punch with its Active Tilt Control (ATC) system.

Using carefully placed sensors, a computer could calculate the tilt of the tandem two-seater body as the Life-Jet entered and progressed through a bend. Using this instant feedback, optimum control could be exerted on the springs by the hydraulic system to shift the center of gravity and ensure it wouldn't overturn.

At very high speeds, minimum body roll would maintain stability, but the set-up would "relax" at lower speeds to let the cockpit lean over to a maximum 30 degrees.

ATC would permit a g-force of 0.9, pretty exhilarating for a typical car driver—no helmet or leathers were required, the seats had belts, and air-conditioning was included.

The aluminum chassis weighed just 196lb (89kg) while the bodyshell and vertically opening front-hinged doors were aircraft-inspired. In good weather, the two roof sections could be removed and stowed in the boot. The Mercedes A-Class engine behind the passengers drove the single rear wheel through a five-speed manual gearbox. A sensor was added to automatically turn on the headlights in ambient light conditions.

## SPECIFICATION

**YEAR REVEALED** 1997

**PLACE OF ORIGIN** Stuttgart, Germany

**HISTORICAL STATUS** prototype

**ENGINE** four-cylinder, 98ci (1,598cc)

**MAXIMUM POWER** 102bhp

**LAYOUT** rear-mounted engine driving the rear wheel

**BODYWORK** two-canopy-door, two-seater coupé

**TOP SPEED** 135mph (217kph)

**NUMBER BUILT** one

*"For a firm renowned for its conservative image, Mercedes pulled out all the stops with the F 300 to produce a design as gloriously irrelevant as possible."*

RICHARD DREDGE IN HIS BOOK *CONCEPT CARS*, 2004

The ATC system allowed a "lean" of up to 30 degrees for authentic motorcycle thrills.

# MCC SMART

The iconic Smart city car has its genesis in watchmaking rather than the automotive world, because the "father" of Smart was Hungarian-born entrepreneur Nicolas Hayek, creator of the cheap and trendy Swatch timepiece credited with reinvigorating Switzerland's watch industry.

Hayek's vision for a "Swatchmobile" featured interchangeable body panels, allowing buyers a wide choice of colors and finishes characteristic of Swatch watches. Original tenets also included pure electric and diesel-electric hybrid power, and a tiny "footprint" so two of the cars would occupy the space of one conventional sedan.

Swatch knew it couldn't build the Smart car alone, however, and Mercedes-Benz became its production partner in the Micro Compact Car project in 1994. The stubby little car was based around what Smart called a Tridion safety cell, an exposed chassis-body frame encircling the cockpit and defining the exterior shape; on to this, the plastic body panels could be attached.

Mercedes-Benz developed a range of turbocharged three-cylinder engines for installation in the rear of the car, and all Smarts would come with a clutch-less transmission that could be driven in fully automatic or manual-shift modes.

The car's stability and effective crumple zones gained the Smart a creditable three-star rating in Euro NCAP crash protection tests. The MCC Smart was unveiled in 1998, but Hayek sold his 19 percent stake in the venture to Mercedes.

## SPECIFICATION

**YEAR REVEALED** 1998

**PLACE OF ORIGIN** Renningen, Germany, and Hambach, France

**HISTORICAL STATUS** production car

**ENGINE** three-cylinder, 37–43ci (599–698cc) gas and 49ci (799cc) diesel

**MAXIMUM POWER** 61bhp

**LAYOUT** rear-mounted engine driving the rear wheels

**BODYWORK** three-door coupé and two-door convertible

**TOP SPEED** 85mph (137kph)

**NUMBER BUILT** 770,256

*"The automotive equivalent of a funky mobile phone complete with snap-on panels to suit your mood. It is narrow enough to slot through places where only despatch riders dare to go."*

BBC *TOP GEAR* MAGAZINE, 2002

The black body sections of this Smart are its Tridion safety cell, while the red areas are the interchangeable panels as envisaged by Nicolas Hayek.

The lifting gear of the X-trem could hoist and deposit its hovercraft and act as a rollover bar if the radical workhorse flipped over.

# RINSPEED X-TREM

Strictly-speaking, the X-Trem is a pickup truck rather than a car. But an open two-seater with an on-board hovercraft would always be a vehicle that transcended boundaries. Since 1979, Switzerland's Rinspeed Design has sought to enliven the motoring world with its way-out productions, but this one went further than most, and was, in Europe, fully road-legal.

The company's principal Frank Rinderknecht said he was impelled to create the X-Trem after noticing how cumbersome the load bays of pickups could be with their high-up flatbeds. To overcome this, he devised his patented multiplex "X-Tra-Lift" device, which could crane up and lower to the ground any item of equipment on board. Not so far removed from the lifting gear on a garbage truck, this was also designed to double as a rollover bar in the event of the X-Trem overturning in an accident.

So the X-Trem could frequent building sites during the week and beaches at the weekend. As "presentation cargo," Rinspeed commissioned one of the smallest ever functional hovercraft from Japanese company Sorex—and the first ever "fitted" to any car.

Rinspeed called it a Multi-Utility Vehicle (MUV). The underpinnings were an extended Mercedes-Benz G-Class chassis, while the frontal styling paid tribute to both Mercedes and Chrysler models. Twin retractable screens shielded driver and passenger, and there was a computer, a cigar humidor, and waterproof upholstery.

## SPECIFICATION

**YEAR REVEALED** 1999

**PLACE OF ORIGIN** Zumikon, Switzerland

**HISTORICAL STATUS** prototype

**ENGINE** V8-cylinder, 332ci (5,439cc)

**MAXIMUM POWER** 347bhp

**LAYOUT** front-mounted engine driving all four wheels

**BODYWORK** doorless, two-seater buggy/utility

**TOP SPEED** 150mph (241kph) (claimed)

**NUMBER BUILT** one

*"This vehicle can now be loaded swiftly, easily, and without effort and therefore can be used in every aspect of life."*

FRANK RINDERKNECHT, 1999

The MUV acronym may not have caught on, but designs were patented anyway.

# TVR SPEED 12

Until its demise in 2006, TVR (from founder TreVoR Wilkinson) manufactured powerful sports cars renowned for their individualistic styling.

At the heart of the Speed 12 was a landmark TVR engine, a 48-valve V12, with a steel block created by joining two six-cylinder engines together on a single crankshaft. With a six-speed gearbox driving the rear wheels, it was installed in a modified TVR race track-only Tuscan chassis.

Known as Project 7/12 (7 liters and 12 cylinders), it made an enormous impact at the 1996 British motor show. On the track,

the TVR also gave a stunning performance, allegedly hitting 60mph (97kph) in under 3 seconds. But the car was a brute to drive, immensely demanding at speed.

TVR attempted to tame the beast, and by 2000, a new car was ready. Weighing just 1 ton (1,000kg) to keep the 231mph (372kph) McLaren F1 within its gunsights, it was renamed Speed 12, and restyled to resemble a pumped-up TVR Cerbera with aerodynamic additions. At £188,000, it would have been the costliest TVR, if company owner Peter Wheeler hadn't axed the car because he felt it was too powerful.

## SPECIFICATION

**YEAR REVEALED**  2000

**PLACE OF ORIGIN**  Blackpool, Lancashire, UK

**HISTORICAL STATUS**  prototype

**ENGINE**  V12-cylinder, 472ci (7,730cc)

**MAXIMUM POWER**  800–960bhp estimated

**LAYOUT**  front-mounted engine driving the rear wheels

**BODYWORK**  two-door, two-seater coupé

**TOP SPEED**  240mph (386kph) (potential)

**NUMBER BUILT**  one

*"Awesome... terrifyingly quick... Even the seating position was crazy; it's like getting into a normal car and then sitting on the floor—in the back."*

JOHN BARKER, *EVO* MAGAZINE, 2005

TVR wanted to drive the Speed 12 at the Le Mans 24-hour race, but that never happened.

# IDEA KAZ

Red carpet evenings in Hollywood will never be the same again if the KAZ, or something like it, ever makes it into mainstream motoring.

The design was outlined by a team at Japan's Keio University headed by Professor Hiroshi Shimizu, who wanted to demonstrate the promise that lithium-ion batteries held for the road. Shimizu decided to incorporate the technology in a stretch limousine. He began work in 1996, and when the result made its entrance at the 2001 Geneva Motor Show, the Keio Advanced Zero-emissions vehicle had cost $4 million.

The eight-wheeled car had an electric motor in the hub of each of its wheels, individually generating 74bhp of power. The 84 lithium-ion batteries—fed through an "Intelligent Power Module" drive unit—were concealed under the floor, making the interior of the KAZ appropriately spacious.

A single charge gave a 186-mile (299-km) range for the KAZ limo. The vehicle was designed in collaboration with, and built by, Italy's I.D.E.A. consultancy, an automotive industry favorite for prototypes, and proved its mettle in October 2002 when it achieved a spectacular 193mph (311kph) at an Italian test track.

Although it never reached production, the Keio designers claimed it could be adaptable as a truck or bus. However, considering the enthusiasm celebrities have for the "green" hybrid Toyota Prius, the KAZ electric limousines would still be the hottest thing possible for LA premieres.

## SPECIFICATION

**YEAR REVEALED** 2001

**PLACE OF ORIGIN** Kanagawa, Japan, and Turin, Italy

**HISTORICAL STATUS** prototype

**ENGINE** eight electric motors

**MAXIMUM POWER** 580bhp equivalent

**LAYOUT** electric motors mounted in wheels

**BODYWORK** six-door, eight-seater limousine

**TOP SPEED** 193mph (311kph)

**NUMBER BUILT** one

*"A lithium-ion battery is widely used for mobile phones—we simply used large-sized lithium-ion batteries. When KAZ succeeded in running at 311kph, it was so fast our photographer couldn't take the picture!"* PROFESSOR HIROSHI SHIMIZU, KAZ PROJECT DIRECTOR, 2002

Six of the Kaz's eight wheels could be steered to turn the giant car.

The Bentley EXP Speed 8 (left) which
won the Le Mans 24-hour race in 2003,
with the ultra desirable Bentley
Continental GT (right).

# RENAULT SPORT CLIO V6

Car manufacturers revere the image-boosting aura of Formula One, but few are able to match this in their showrooms. However, Renault found a novel way to fuse Grand Prix machine with suburban shopping car in its amazing Clio V6.

Instead of squeezing a tuned 227bhp Renaultsport V6 power unit under the hood of a normal front-wheel drive Clio, Renault removed the back seats, and positioned the engine transversely between the rear wheels. The resulting car looked outwardly normal, but boasted race car-style handling and high performance.

Although the inner shell, roof, hood and boot were shared with other Clios, the V6 was almost entirely new underneath its flamboyantly flared wheelarch side pods.

With luggage space stolen by the engine, and heavy gas consumption, it wasn't practical; instead, here was a two-seater car with scintillating handling, despite tricky slippery-road traction and poor steering lock. The V6 and six-speed gearbox installation entailed such major reworking that the car weighed 661lb (300kg) more than the most powerful "ordinary" Clio, the 172 Cup, with similar acceleration.

Renault conceived the V6 in 1998, and contracted its development to race team TWR who engineered it in the UK and hand-built it in Sweden. When the main Clio range was updated stylistically in 2003, so was the V6, also seeing its power upped to 252bhp and suspension realigned to tame its hairy waywardness.

## SPECIFICATION

**YEAR REVEALED** 2000

**PLACE OF ORIGIN** Uddevalla, Sweden, and Paris/Dieppe, France

**HISTORICAL STATUS** production car

**ENGINE** V6-cylinder, 180ci (2,946cc)

**MAXIMUM POWER** 252bhp

**LAYOUT** rear/mid-mounted engine driving the rear wheels

**BODYWORK** three-door, two-seater hatchback

**TOP SPEED** 153mph (246kph)

**NUMBER BUILT** 866

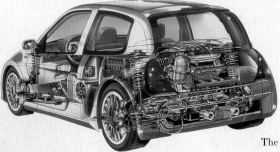

*"You have to concentrate 100 percent... This isn't a car for hooligans, but it is an intoxicating challenge."*

REVIEW IN *EVO* MAGAZINE, 2007

The 180ci (2,946cc) V6 was crammed into the Clio's trunk space.

The silhouette of the old lady's shopping car remains, but the flared contours of the Sport Clio V6 hint at the fire-breathing monster within.

The Bentley's back "suicide doors" are hinged at the rear and can open at right angles to ensure elegant and easy access.

# BENTLEY STATE LIMOUSINE

The golden jubilee of Queen Elizabeth II, in 2002, was cause for rejoicing around the UK, with ceremonial events and street parties. The country's auto industry perhaps lacked the empirical stature it enjoyed when Her Majesty acceded to the throne in 1952, but a Bentley-led consortium was still determined to create a suitable commemorative gift for her: a new state limousine.

Bentley badge

This was a unique, one-off car for ceremonial duties, and was designed in close collaboration with Buckingham Palace. For instance, the floor of the rear compartment was high enough for the transmission tunnel to be positioned unobtrusively beneath, with wide-opening doors cut into the roof of the monocoque body allowing the monarch to stand upright when disembarking. The Royal household chose black-over-Royal Claret paintwork with red coachlines, requesting minimum external chrome, and comfortable trim and upholstery.

This timeless Bentley—which runs on liquid-gaseum fuel—was presented to the queen in May 2002. At that time, Bentley and Rolls-Royce were being de-merged after having spent 71 years as one company; Bentley was acquired by German car maker Volkswagen. The limousine arrived 25 years after the queen had been presented with a modified Rolls-Royce Phantom VI for her silver jubilee in 1977.

## SPECIFICATION

**YEAR REVEALED** 2002

**PLACE OF ORIGIN** Crewe, Cheshire, UK

**HISTORICAL STATUS** bespoke ceremonial limousine

**ENGINE** V8-cylinder, 412ci (6,750cc)

**MAXIMUM POWER** 400bhp

**LAYOUT** front-mounted engine driving the rear wheels

**BODYWORK** four-door, six-seater limousine

**TOP SPEED** unknown

**NUMBER BUILT** one

*"I was lucky to be given almost total freedom to style the car the way I wanted… From a designer's point of view, it was the dream job."*

CRISPIN MARSHFIELD, SENIOR DESIGNER OF THE
BENTLEY STATE LIMOUSINE, SPEAKING IN 2002

# ENZO FERRARI

The name of this vehicle is a tribute to the man who founded the fabulous Ferrari marque. Enzo Ferrari himself died in 1988, but his company—and its incredibly successful Formula One team—have continued to flourish.

The two-seater Enzo Ferrari drew heavy inspiration from Formula One champion Michael Schumacher's racing machines. Like a Formula One car, the Enzo had a carbon-fiber-composite monocoque structure, body panels made from CFC/Nomex, and a V12 engine. However, while the racing Ferrari featured wind-cheating wings and baffles, the Enzo Ferrari relied on a cunning "active aerodynamics" system.

Ferrari badge

At the front, it sported a Formula-One style raised nose and two massive air intakes to channel air up to the brakes and over the windshield. The tail section was abruptly truncated but had no rear aerofoil; instead, huge venturis between the rear wheels sucked out air, pulling the car down hard to the road surface. It had carbon-ceramic brakes discs, too. Ferrari's traditional design partner Pininfarina was commissioned to style the car. The lithe, aggressive supercar, with a functional cockpit lined with carbon fiber, hit the bullseye. Within hours of launch, all 349 Enzos were sold at £425,000 apiece, and Ferrari agreed to build 51 more only after uproar from frustrated collectors.

## SPECIFICATION

**YEAR REVEALED** 2002

**PLACE OF ORIGIN** Maranello, Modena, Italy

**HISTORICAL STATUS** production car

**ENGINE** V12-cylinder, 366ci (5,998cc)

**MAXIMUM POWER** 660bhp

**LAYOUT** mid-mounted engine driving the rear wheels

**BODYWORK** two-door, two-seater coupé

**TOP SPEED** 217mph (349kph)

**NUMBER BUILT** 400

*"Steering is fantastic, quick, direct, perfectly weighted. But above it all is that engine. The Enzo accelerates so fiercely [that] the next corner comes rushing up to the windshield."*

JOE LORIO, *AUTOMOBILE* MAGAZINE, 2002

Active aerodynamics, a body/chassis made of carbon fiber, and carbon-ceramic brakes featured in this stunning tribute to the founder of Ferrari.

The ZEN was a fusion of modern automotive technology and Japanese traditions of serenity, yet came from Birmingham rather than Tokyo.

# ISUZU ZEN

Whimsical concepts are a Japanese thing. The biennial Tokyo Motor Show is usually crammed with them—the event is often more like a design student's degree exhibition than a serious prophesy of the automotive future. Isuzu's ZEN is a prime example of this left-field ideas forum.

The only thing is, it wasn't created in Japan at all, but at Isuzu's European design center in the UK. The premise was to package some tranquil Japanese-style living space within the proportions of a typical delivery van. Why any driver might want this wasn't clear, but Isuzu talked of it as mobile office space or, for crowded Japanese cities where offspring often live at home with their parents, an annex-on-wheels for meditation, tea, even passion.

Chief designer Geoffrey Gardner trawled the modern art collection of London's Tate Modern gallery for inspiration to mix with Zen Buddhist principles of harmony, respect, and purity. Viewed side-on, the nose section housed the turbodiesel engine; the passenger compartment resembled a radiating Japanese paper fan; and the cargo cube was tacked on the end.

The "Transformer"-style interior converted into a serene traditional Japanese tearoom, with bamboo flooring and tatami woven mats, by folding the steering wheel and the silk-covered, aluminum-and-wood front seats away into the dashboard. Other signature touches included the opaque roof light and lower tailgate panel sliding upwards to reveal a view of the outdoors.

## SPECIFICATION

**YEAR REVEALED** 2001

**PLACE OF ORIGIN** Birmingham, West Midlands, UK, and Tokyo, Japan

**HISTORICAL STATUS** prototype

**ENGINE** V6-cylinder, 183ci (2,999cc) diesel

**MAXIMUM POWER** unknown

**LAYOUT** front-mounted engine driving all four wheels

**BODYWORK** two-door, four-seater station wagon

**TOP SPEED** unknown

**NUMBER BUILT** one

*"The effects of incorporating Japanese architecture and culture into the ZEN looks fantastic."*

STEPHEN NEWBURY, *THE CAR DESIGN YEARBOOK 1, 2002*

# BUGATTI VEYRON

Bugatti's Veyron is not the very latest supercar we could have chosen to conclude this journey through 120 years of extraordinary automobiles. But it is highly appropriate as a truly grand finale. Because the Veyron is still the fastest accelerating—0–62mph (0–100kph) in 2.46 seconds—production road car ever seen. And the most expensive of all time. With exactly 987bhp, it's one of a tiny handful of so-called "standard" models to get anywhere near a four-figure power output, and with the second-highest ever top speed.

Volkswagen acquired the revered Bugatti brand in 1998, and resolved to do something spectacular with it, but it took until 2005 to build the factory and finalize the car itself; the Veyron 16.4. Mounted centrally was something never seen before in any car: a W16 engine with four banks of four cylinders—the equivalent of two V8 engines joined together. This puts its amazing power, boosted by four turbochargers, to the road via a sequential seven-speed gearbox and four-wheel drive. There are a grand total of ten radiators to keep the car cool.

The price for all this, plus fastidious hand-built quality, is a quoted €1.1m. But Volkswagen will make scant profit on its huge investment in making its new Bugatti a truly ultimate car. The vindication is that the Veyron has been independently proven to reach its 253mph (407kph) maximum speed. Active aerodynamics deploy automatically at 137mph (220kph) and "everyday" top speed is limited to 233mph (375kph).

## SPECIFICATION

**YEAR REVEALED** 2005

**PLACE OF ORIGIN** Molsheim, Alsace, France

**HISTORICAL STATUS** production car

**ENGINE** W16-cylinder, 7,993cc (488ci)

**MAXIMUM POWER** 987bhp

**LAYOUT** mid-mounted engine driving all four wheels

**BODYWORK** two-door, two-seater station wagon

**TOP SPEED** 407kph (253mph)

**NUMBER BUILT** 300

*"From behind the wheel of a Veyron, France is the size of a small coconut. I cannot tell you how fast I crossed it the other day. It is a triumph for lunacy over common sense."*

BBC2 *TOP GEAR'S* JEREMY CLARKSON IN *THE SUNDAY TIMES*, 2005

A landmark in car engine design was reached with the Veyron's 488ci (7,993cc) W16.

This is the pre-production Veyron that drew the crowds at the 2004 Paris Motor Show: crowned the world's fastest, most-expensive motor car ever.

# INDEX

This is the pre-production Veyron that drew the crowds at the 2004 Paris Motor Show: crowned the world's fastest, most-expensive motor car ever.

# INDEX

# ACKNOWLEDGMENTS

## AUTHOR'S ACKNOWLEDGMENTS

Over 25 years, countless people have helped me accumulate the facts and pictures in this book, but I'd like to thank the following individuals who have been kind enough to contribute their help to this one specifically: Neill Bruce & the late Peter Roberts; Alan Stote and Red Triangle Autoservices, who kindly supplied the Alvis picture on page 51/52; David Tremayne; Robin Davies at Audi UK; Stephen Vokins & Patrick Collins at the National Motor Museum, Beaulieu; Devie Davison; Mike Lawrence; Simon Taylor; Tom Candlish; Janette Green & Kevin Watters at Aston Martin Lagonda; Sarah Shortt at McLaren Group; Richard and Vicky Dredge; Debbie Hull at Smart; Jason Harris at Ferrari GB. My wife Annabel and son Spencer need thanks too, for putting up with—and supporting—an occasionally grumpy author.

**GILES CHAPMAN** is an award-winning writer and commentator on the industry, history, and culture of cars. He began his career in 1984 in automotive consultancy, moving into magazine publishing in 1985. By 1991, he was editor of *Classic & Sports Car*, the world's best-selling classic car magazine. Since 1994, he's worked freelance across a huge variety of media. Today, he contributes to national newspapers and motoring publications, and was voted Jeep Consumer Journalist Of The Year in 2005. He's the author of more than a dozen books including *Moving Objects* (co-written with Stephen Bayley), *Chapman's Car Compendium*, and *My Dad Had One Of Those* (co-written with BBC *Top Gear*'s Richard Porter), a non-fiction hardback best-seller in 2007.

## PICTURE CREDITS

The publisher would like to thank the following for their kind permission to reproduce their photographs:

DK Images: Courtesy of American 50s Car Hire 120–121; Tom Turkington c/o Hendon Way Motors 202–203; Roger Wait, Backwell Bristol 260–261; Getty Images: Fox Photos 2; FPG 96–97, 164–165; Keystone 68–69; RacingOne 277; The Kobal Collection: Warfield/United Artists 256; LAT Photographic: 24–25; James Mann: 8–9, 58–59, 302–303; National Motor Museum: 13, 35, 38, 45, 52, 65, 82, 122, 149, 181, 204, 207, 210, 220, 239, 270, 306, 325, 351, 352, 353; Nicky Wright 23, 180

All other images supplied by the Giles Chapman Picture Library

**DATE DUE**

| | | | |
|---|---|---|---|
| | | | |
| | | | |
| | | | |
| | | | |
| | | | |
| | | | |
| | | | |
| | | | |
| | | | |
| | | | |
| | | | |
| | | | |
| | | | |
| | | | |
| | | | |
| | | | |
| | | | |
| GAYLORD | | | PRINTED IN U.S.A. |